STARS & STRIPES
★ FOREVER ★
THE HISTORY OF OUR FLAG

Edited by

John Winthrop Adams

SMITHMARK

Page 1: The golden morning sunlight touches Our Flag.

Pages 2-3: Old Glory, adopted in 1777 with 13 stars in its blue field, evolved to its present 50-star configuration in 1960.

This page: Our Flag flies proudly between the twin towers of the Vietnam Memorial and from the Florida state capitol in Tallahassee. Florida was the 27th state admitted to the Union, the 27th star added to the flag.

This edition published in 1992 by SMITHMARK Publishers Inc. 112 Madison Avenue New York, New York 10016

SMITHMARK books are available for bulk purchase for sales promotion and premium use. For details write or telephone the Manager of Special Sales, SMITHMARK Publishers Inc., 112 Madison Avenue, New York, NY 10016. (212) 532-6600.

Produced by Brompton Books Corp., 15 Sherwood Place, Greenwich, CT 06830.

ISBN 0-8317-6658-1

Printed in Hong Kong

10 9 8 7 6 5 4 3 2 1

Photo credits

American Graphic Systems Archives endpapers, 16 top, 27
Anne SK Brown Military Collection, Brown University 9
Bibliotheque Nationale via Brompton Books 6, 7
Bison Picture Library 8 top
Michael Clark via Vermont Travel Division 58
William Clark via National Park Service 47
Ruth DeJauregui 51 both, 67
Terry Farms via Illinois Department of Commerce and Community Affairs 13 top
Florida Department of Commerce, Division of Tourism 4, 54 bottom
Girl Scouts USA 32 both
Tom Hindman, Maine Office of Tourism via American Graphic Systems 27
Illinois Department of Commerce and Community Affairs 1, 13 bottom, 64, 76
S Jameson via Florida Department of Commerce, Division of Tourism 63
NASA 36 both, 37, 40 top, 41
National Archives 18, 24, 28, 29, 31, 34, 35, 48, 50, 57, 60, 69
National Gallery of Art 15
Smithsonian Institution 11, 21
Tennessee Department of Tourism 55
US Department of Defense 30, 40 bottom, 54 top, 65, 68
US Marine Corps 43
US Military Academy 45
US Navy 14, 17, 25, 26
The White House 44, 48
Wisconsin Division of Tourism 46
© Bill Yenne cover, 16 bottom, 19, 33, 38, 39, 49, 52, 53, 56, 61, 70, 71, 72-73, 74-75, 79, 80

Designed by Bill Yenne

TABLE OF CONTENTS

THE HERITAGE OF OUR FLAG

Below: This battle scene from the Hundred Years' War depicts cavalry versus foot soldiers. Each army bears the emblems of their native lands. The gold on blue Bourbon flag of France was one of the first flags to fly over what is now the United States of America.

As early as the thirteenth century, standards such as those *opposite* were carried by a Sultan's guards. These were the precursors of the flags which are, in turn, the precursors of today's national flags.

S omewhere in the mists of prehistory, humankind first selected a special symbol by which a person or tribe could be distinguished from others. These images, which anthropologists call *totems*, became the tribal symbols which over time developed into the emblems distinctive of nations. Eventually these took the form of the insignia from which we derive our flags.

The earliest national symbols were ordinary images or badges wrought in metal, stone or wood, and carried at the top of a pole or spear. Thus, Egypt marched to war beneath the sacred emblems of their gods or the fan of feathers of the pharaohs, while the Assyrian insignia was a circular disc bearing a running bull or two bulls tail to tail. Both of these often also had a small streamer attached to the staff immediately below the device. These were probably the first flags. The Greeks also used symbols of their deities, such as the owl of Athens, or legendary animals, like the pegasus of Corinth, the minotaur of Crete or the tortoise of the Peloponnesus. Homer suggests that Agamemnon used a purple veil as a rallying signal.

The sculptures of Persepolis show us that the Persians adopted the figures of the sun, the eagle and the like, which in time were replaced by the blacksmith's apron. For the Romans, the figure of a horse or wolf or other animal was used until a lone eagle was adopted by the emperor Marius. Pliny writes that, in his second consulship, Marius ordered that the Roman legions

A la Journee de frouuignu   ver faint clement pour

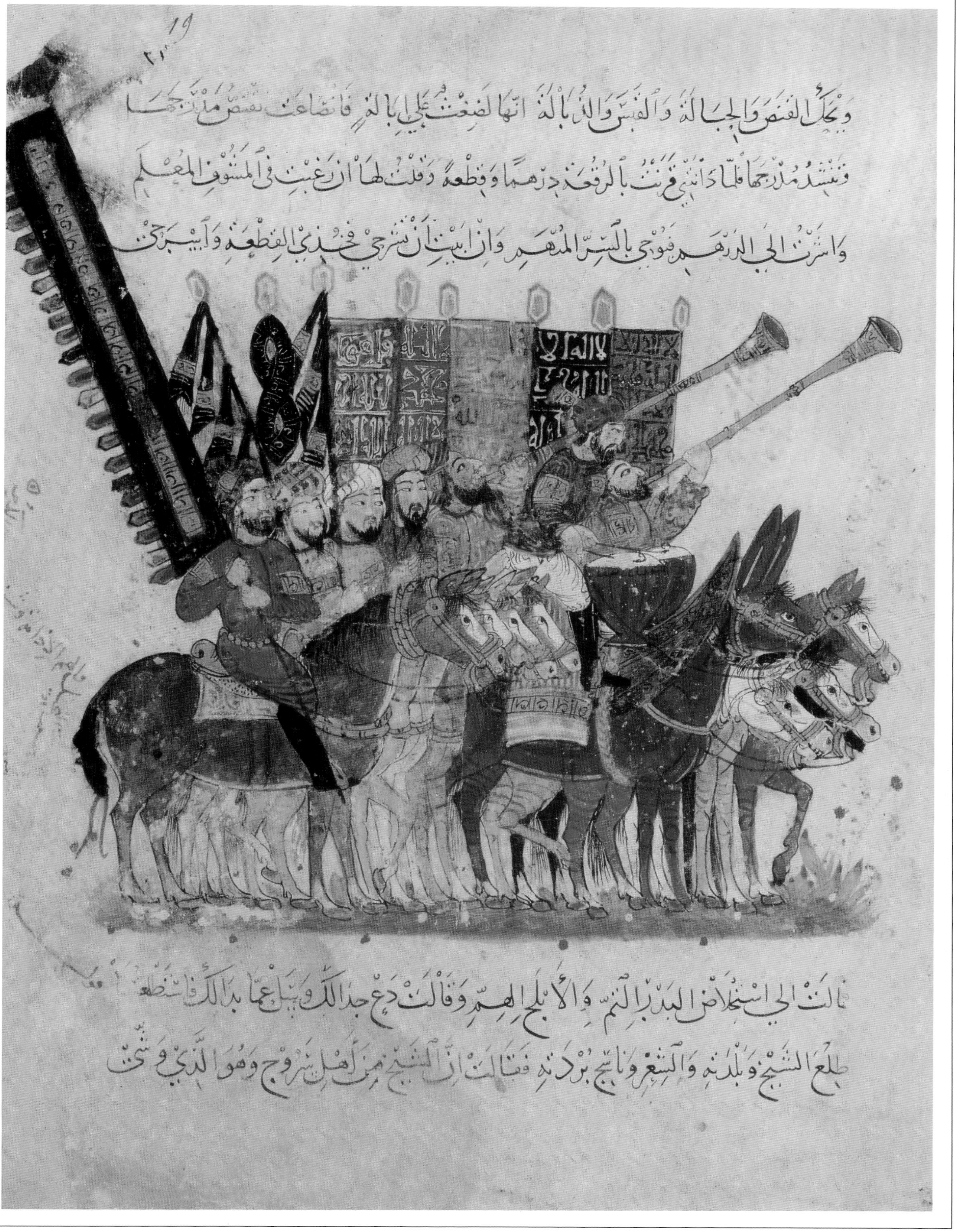

Above: Henry VII of England as St George, standing on the vanquished dragon and holding a flag with the red cross of St George, the ensign of England.

Below: The flag of England (*top*) with the cross of St George was combined with the flag of Scotland (*bottom*) with the cross of St Andrew to form the Union Jack of Great Britain.

Opposite: The Union Jack flies from a British warship at Cape Breton Island in 1745. At first Britain's Union Jack was used primarily as a naval ensign.

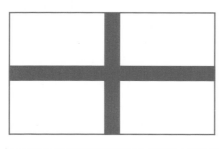

should have the eagle only as their standard. 'For before that time, the eagle marched foremost with four others, wolves, minotaurs, horses and bears, each one in its proper order. Not many years passed before the eagle alone began to be in advance and the rest left behind in the camp. But Marius rejected them altogether, and since then, there has rarely been a camp of a legion in winter quarters without a pair of eagles.'

Meanwhile, there were other insignia. According to Livy, the Roman vexillum, or cavalry flag, was a square piece of textile material fixed to a crossbar at the end of a spear, often richly fringed, and either plain or with devices, and was undoubtedly a flag.

The insignia which distinguished the allied forces from the Roman legions, were also more or less flags, as may be seen on the columns of Trajan and Antonine, the arch of Titus and in many coins and medals of ancient Rome. Later, the Romans adopted for their auxiliaries the dragon of Parthia, which in time became the standard of the Emperors of the West, and which can be said to be the origin of the golden dragon of Wessex and the red dragon of Wales.

The Union Jack of Britain

The first reference to banners in England is in Bede's description of the interview between King Ethelbert and St Augustine, wherein the followers of the latter are said to have borne 'a silver cross for a banner'—clearly showing that banners were then in use, but St Augustine did not have one. Banners of this type were formerly part of the usual ornaments of the altar, and are still largely used to add to the pomp of religious processions. Ecclesiastical flags were often purely pictorial in character, being actual representations of the Trinity, the Madonna or different saints. At other times, the religious houses bore banners heraldic in character, as the chiefs of the church were lords temporal, in respect of many of their possessions, as well as lords spiritual, and took their places among the fighting men at the head of the retainers they were required to maintain in aid of the national defense. In these cases, the distinguishing banner of the contingent obviously conformed to the banners of the respective dukes or barons.

Heraldic and political devices on flags came later, but even when these came freely into vogue they did not supplant ecclesiastical symbols. The banners of the original orders of knighthood belong to the religious group. That of the Knights Hospitalers was a silver cross on a black field. The Templars carried a banner that was black over white horizontal, which they called Breauset 'because they were fair and favorable to the friends of Christ but black and terrible to his enemies.' The Teutonic Knights bore the black cross on a white field, which survives in the twentieth century as the Iron Cross of Germany. It was in use in West Germany from 1949 to 1991, and in unified Germany since.

The national banner of England—the red cross of her patron, St George—was for centuries a religious one. Whatever other banners were carried, this would be the first in the field. The royal banner of Great Britain and Ireland, in its rich blazonry of the lions of England and Scotland and the Irish harp, is a good example of the heraldic flag, while the current Union Jack similarly symbolizes the three components of the United Kingdom by the allied crosses, two of which are the old crosses of St George and St Andrew, the third being the saltire assigned to St Patrick in the seventeenth century.

In 1245 on St George's Day, Frederick II instituted an order of knighthood and placed it under the guardianship of that soldier saint. Its white banner, bearing the red cross, floated in battle alongside that of the German Empire. On St George's Day in 1350, Edward III of England instituted the Order of the Garter. By the fourteenth century, the cross of St George was worn as a distinctive mark on a surcoat, over the armor, by every English soldier.

The Cross of St Andrew is shaped like the letter 'X,' representing the two pieces of timber driven into the ground to which the saint was tied instead of being nailed. Legend asserts that this form of cross appeared in the sky to Achaius, King of the Scots, the night before the great battle with Athelstan. Having been victorious, Achaius went barefoot to the church of St Andrew and vowed to adopt his cross as the Scottish national emblem.

The joining of the two kingdoms of England and Scotland—henceforth known as Great Britain—into one under the sovereignty of King James, necessitated a new design for the flag to typify this union which would blend together the emblems of the two patron saints. The Royal Ordinance of 12 April 1605 states: 'Whereas some difference hath arisen between our

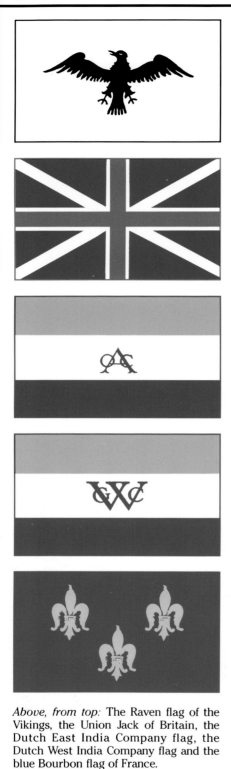

Above, from top: The Raven flag of the Vikings, the Union Jack of Britain, the Dutch East India Company flag, the Dutch West India Company flag and the blue Bourbon flag of France.

Opposite: Christopher Columbus arrived in the New World on 12 October 1492 under the Royal Standard of Spain, a flag whose colors would be a familiar sight in the western hemisphere for the next several centuries.

subjects of South and North Britain, traveling by seas, about the bearing of their flags, for the avoiding of all such contentions hereafter, we have, with the advice of our Council, ordered that from henceforth all our subjects of this isle and kingdom of Greater Britain, and its members hereof, shall bear in their maintop the Red Cross, commonly called St George's Cross, and the White Cross, commonly called St Andrew's Cross, joined together, according to a form made by our Heralds, and sent by us to our Admiral to be published to our said subjects.'

The first mention of the composition of the current Union Jack was made in the Order of the King in Council of 5 November 1800. The immediate use of the flag was required by the following proclamation of 1 January 1801: 'Whereas by the First Article of the Articles of Union of Great Britain and Ireland it was declared: That the said kingdoms of Great Britain and Ireland should upon this day, being the first day of January in the Year of our Lord One Thousand Eight Hundred and One, for ever after be united into one kingdom, by the name of the United Kingdom of Great Britain and Ireland, and that the Royal Style and Titles appertaining to the Imperial Crown of the said United Kingdom and its dependencies, and also the ensigns armorial, flags and banners thereof, should be such as we, by our Royal Proclamation under the Great Seal of the said United Kingdom, should appoint… and that the Union Flag shall be azure, the Crosses Saltire of St Andrew and St Patrick quarterly, per Saltire counterchanged Argent and Gules: the latter fimbriated of the second, surmounted by the Cross of St George of the third, fimbriated as the Saltire.'

The Earliest European Flags in North America

In the year 1000—nearly 500 years before the landing of Columbus—a crew of Vikings, under Leif Ericson, visited the Atlantic seacoast of North America, sailing as far south as present-day Narragansett Bay, Rhode Island, where they spent the winter. Theirs was the first European flag to fly over the continent of North America.

When going to sea, the Vikings generally took ravens with them. When in doubt which way to steer, they would liberate a raven, which would fly in the direction of land, and the ship would follow its flight. The raven became the emblem of the Vikings and was placed on their banners. This had precedence with the Danes, who, as early as 878, carried the raven, at first as an image and then as a flag. Theirs was a small, triangular banner with fringe, bearing a black raven on a blood-red field. The Viking banner of 1000 was a black raven on a rectangular white field.

The banner that Columbus planted when he landed at San Salvador on 12 October 1492 was the Royal Standard of Spain. It had a red field on which there appeared a castle, the insignia of the province of Castile, and a white field with a red lion, the emblem of the province of Leon. A similar banner was carried by Ponce de Leon when he visited Florida in 1512 in search of the magical 'fountain of youth.' Such a flag was also carried by Balboa when he crossed the Isthmus of Panama, reaching the shores of the Pacific Ocean on 7 September 1513, and by DeSoto, during his explorations in the south and the Mississippi Valley in 1539 to 1541.

The next flag flown on the American continent was the English ensign, white with red cross, hoisted there by John Cabot in 1497 on his voyage of discovery for King Henry VII of England. The King's Colors or Grand Union Flag of Great Britain, with the red Cross of St George and the white Scottish Cross of St Andrew, was probably flown from the main topmasts of the *Constant* and the *Mayflower* to Jamestown in 1607 and to Plymouth in 1620, while the Royal Standard of England was flown from their foremasts.

In 1609, Henry Hudson arrived in the *Half Moon* in New Amsterdam (New York) Harbor under the flag of the Dutch East India Company, which had orange, white and blue horizontal fields with the letters VOCA (Vereenigde Oost-Indische Compagnie, Amsterdam) in the white stripe. In 1621, the letters were replaced by the monogram of the Dutch West India Company, GWC (Gevetroijeerde West-Indische Compagnie), the 'G' being on the left outer bar of the 'W,' and the 'C' on the right. In 1638, the blue with the yellow cross of the Swedes who founded New Sweden on the banks of the Delaware was flown, which was superseded by the Dutch in 1655, as the Dutch were in turn mastered by the British by the transformation of New Amsterdam to New York in 1644.

In 1524, Verrazano explored the Atlantic coast, from North Carolina to Newfoundland, sailing under the Blue Bourbon Flag of France, which had three yellow fleurs-de-lys on a blue field. It was also under the blue Bourbon Flag that the famous French

Above, from top: Some of America's early flags: The Taunton Flag (1774), The Bunker Hill Flag (1775), The 'Appeal! to Heaven' Pine Tree Flag of 1776, The Rhode Island Battle Flag (1775), The Fort Moultrie Flag (1775) and New York's naval ensign (1775).

Facing page: The Illinois Lincoln Festival features flags of that era and today.

explorer Jacques Cartier made three voyages to the New World, from 1534 to 1545, during which period he explored the St Lawrence Gulf and River.

On 5 May 1634, Charles I restricted the use of the Union Jack to the Royal Navy, and the national flags of England and Scotland were used for public departments and the merchant services.

The two kingdoms continued under separate administration and separate flags until 1 May 1707. When in 1643 the colonies of Plymouth, Massachusetts Bay, Connecticut and New Haven became the United

Early Colonial Flags

As noted above, before the Continental Congress adopted a flag for the United States, banners of various designs were used in the Colonies. The Bedford Flag included an arm covered with mail extending from a cloud, the hand clasping a sword. Inscribed on a scroll was the motto, *Vince Aut Morire* (Conquer or Die). The three spheres that were included were supposed to represent cannon balls. This banner was destined to have the honor of being the first flag of the American Revolution to receive a baptism of British fire. It was carried at the battles of Lexington and Concord and by the Minutemen of Bedford on 19 April 1775, when,

> By the rude bridge that arched the
>   flood
> Their flag to April's breeze unfurled
> Here once the embattled farmer stood
> And fired the shot heard round the
>   world.

One of the earliest Colonial flags was the Taunton Flag, which was first unfurled at Taunton, Massachusetts in 1774. It was, in reality, the Meteor Flag of England with the word 'Liberty' in large white letters across the lower part of the red field. In New England, 'Pine Tree' Flags were very popular. The pine tree was seen as symbolizing the hardiness of the New Englanders. One such design, known as the Bunker Hill Flag, which was carried by Colonial troops at the Battle of Bunker Hill on 17 June 1775, consisted of a blue field with a white canton bearing the red Cross of St George and a green pine tree. Another well-known flag consisted of a white field with a pine tree, above which were the words 'An Appeal to Heaven.' It was used by the ships of the American Navy in New England waters.

The flag of Rhode Island, adopted in 1775, had 13 white stars in a blue canton and, in a white field, an anchor above which there was a scroll bearing the word

Colonies of New England, their flag, as colonies of England, was the St George's ensign with the royal crown and king's cipher in the center, just as it would have been St Andrew's ensign with a similar crowned cipher if they had been Scottish, as was Nova Scotia. Boston, however, did not part with its pine tree flag for local purposes. When the eighteenth century opened, many of the other colonies had begun to fly flags of their own to distinguish their vessels from one another, and these were the forerunners of the present state flags.

'Hope.' Rhode Islanders would later proudly maintain that the 13 stars in the eventual flag of the United States were suggested by the stars in the flag of Rhode Island. However, the first United States Flag had the stars in a *circular* motif, while in the Rhode Island Flag they appeared in alternating horizontal rows of three and two. It is interesting to note that the middle vertical and horizontal lines of the three stars can be seen to form the Cross of St George, and that the two diagonal lines of five stars form the Cross of St Andrew. Whether this occurred through coincidence or design is not known.

The Moultrie 'Liberty' Flag, first flown in 1775, was the earliest displayed in the South. It was a blue flag with a white crescent in the upper right-hand corner. A year later the word 'Liberty' was added. This was the flag that Sergeant Jasper so gallantly rescued on 28 June 1776 after the British fleet attacked Fort Sullivan at Charleston, South Carolina. When, in recognition of his gallantry, the governor presented him with his own sword and offered him a lieutenant's commission, the sergeant, who could neither read nor write, declined the promotion, saying, 'Sir, I am not fit to keep the company of officers.'

In the South, various designs of a 'Rattlesnake' Flag rivaled the popularity of the Pine Tree Flag in New England. It has been written that Benjamin Franklin defended the rattlesnake symbol on the grounds that the rattlesnake is found only in North America, and that among the ancients, serpents were considered to possess wisdom and vigilance. He added that the rattlesnake does not attack without first giving warning and the number of rattles increase with age. As such, the symbol was especially appropriate for the expected growth of the United States.

One Rattlesnake Flag design, which was known as the Gadsden Flag, consisted of a yellow field with a coiled rattlesnake in the center, under which appeared the words 'Don't Tread on Me.' It was designed by Colonel Christopher Gadsden of South Carolina, who requested that it be used as the flag of the Commander-in-Chief of the American Navy. Congress declined his request, but Commodore Esek Hopkins, in command of the Navy, did fly it as his personal flag on the *Alfred*. The Navy liked Gadsden's idea, and the first Navy ensign adopted in 1775 was a flag having 13 alternate red and white stripes, with a rattlesnake diagonally across eight of the stripes.

When the Revolutionary War began, there was an immediate boom in the making of flags. Massachusetts had its Pine Tree Flag, New York its black beaver on a white field, South Carolina had its handsome silver crescent on blue and Rhode Island had the blue anchor of hope. None, however, could, without arousing jealousies, be adopted as a national flag.

Above: Colonel Christopher Gadsden's rattlesnake flag of 1775 featured the admonition 'Don't Tread On Me.'

THE CREATION OF OUR FLAG

O n 13 December 1775, there was a dinner party attended by George Washington, Benjamin Franklin and other Colonial leaders. Talk turned to the flag question, and the conversation continued until Franklin made a suggestion. 'While the field of our flag must be new in the details of its design, it need not be entirely new in its elements. There is already in use a flag with which the English government is familiar, and which it has not only recognized, but also protected for more than half a century, the design of which can be readily modified, or rather extended, so as to most admirably

Above: The Continental Navy's 10-gun sloop *Sachem* flying the Cambridge Flag, which was adopted officially by George Washington at Cambridge, Massachusetts on New Year's Day in 1775.

Facing page: The father of Our Country, George Washington was also the father of Our Flag. He suffered a lot of criticism for his acceptance of the Union Jack in the Cambridge Flag and went back to the drawing board later in the year. The result would spring to life in Betsy Ross's cutting room in Philadelphia in June 1776.

suit our purpose. I refer to the flag of the East India Company, which is one with a field of alternate longitudinal red and white stripes and having the Cross of St George for a union.' [The East India Company had been in existence for more than 150 years, and at the union of England and Scotland in 1707, the upper canton of the company's flag was changed from the Cross of St George to the union of the Crosses of St George and St Andrew. This canton was in fact the prototype of the current Union Jack.]

Franklin's proposal was received with enthusiasm, and on 1 January 1776, 20 days after the dinner, Washington hoisted this national flag at Prospect Hill near Cambridge, Massachusetts. It consisted of 13 alternate red and white stripes with the Union Jack in the canton. It was variously designated as the Union Flag, the Grand Union Flag and the Great Union Flag, and is now occasionally referred to as the Cambridge Flag.

This flag obviously had a drawback in the fact that the Union Jack was included, and the Grand Union Flag was not very well received. The stripes were acceptable—nothing could be better—but there was a lot of debate over what should replace the Union Jack in the upper canton. To take away the red cross they would take away England but leave the white Cross of St Andrew, which was just as objectionable. The Liberty Tree was suggested, but green on white was not agreeable.

Enter Mrs Betsy Ross

Above: On the morning of her delivery of the first Flag, Betsy Ross paused to demonstrate her technique for quickly cutting a five-pointed star.

Below: Betsy Ross's Philadelphia home still flies a 13-star Flag.

Perhaps one of the most compelling and enigmatic of the stories surrounding the birth of the American Flag is that of Elizabeth Griscom Ross. She was born in Philadelphia on New Year's Day 1752, the daughter of devout Quakers Samuel Griscom and Rebecca James. In 1773, she married John Ross, an upholsterer's apprentice and the son of Reverend Aneas Ross, an Episcopal clergyman. The idea of Betsy not marrying a Quaker displeased her parents, but the newlyweds settled into a good life together, opening a small upholstery shop in their home at 89 Arch Street in Philadelphia.

After the battles of Lexington and Concord in April 1775, war clouds began to gather, and John Ross enlisted in the Pennsylvania militia. Fortunately, John was stationed near Philadelphia, but his duties so preoccupied him that Betsy had to take full charge of their shop. On the snowy, miserable afternoon of 21 January, Betsy was hard at work when a friend came to call. Betsy began a cheery greeting, but something in her friend's face stopped her short. There had been an accident, he told her—an explosion of gunpowder on the wharf. Wide-eyed, she looked at him, incredulous. Fear suddenly reached down into her heart, for beyond him in the street, their uniforms grayed by the falling sleet, she saw a group of militiamen carrying toward her the broken, bleeding and unconscious form of John Ross. He never regained consciousness, and was buried at nearby Christ Church.

Barely 24 years old and disowned by her family for marrying outside her faith, Betsy Ross found herself a widow with the sole responsibility of a business. Ironically, it had been on her twenty-fourth birthday three weeks before that Washington had first flown the Grand Union Flag. The never-popular Grand Union continued to be superseded by the Moultrie Flag, the Gadsden Flag and many others, and many people believed there was still a serious need for a unique national American Flag.

At the end of May, Washington came to Philadelphia to discuss the defense of the city, and once again, the flag issue was in the forefront of discussion. As legend has it, Washington was in a meeting with Robert Morris, the patriot financier and chairman of the secret committee on military supplies, and Colonel George Ross (no relation) of Delaware, when he decided that the time of procrastination was over. Something had to be done, and done *now*. John Hancock had mentioned there was an upholstery shop near his home at Fourth and Arch, so Washington seized his hat and was out the door, with Ross and Morris rushing to keep up.

Betsy Ross, having put away the breakfast dishes in her basement kitchen, was getting ready for a busy day in the shop when the three gentlemen appeared at her door. Dropping her work, she stepped forward to admit them. To her surprise, she recognized the faces of Robert Morris, Colonel Ross and, beside him, too astounding for belief, stood the tall, unmistakable figure of General George Washington.

Colonel Ross quickly explained to the young widow the nature of their visit. She led the way back through the crowded shop to her living room. Like so many dwellings of the time, the ground floor of her home had two rooms. At the front was the shop. At the rear, reached by a small connecting hallway with painted walls and

a white, sanded floor, was the sitting room, which also did duty on formal occasions as a dining room.

It was not the first time, by any means, that she had seen Washington, but probably the very first time she had been in his presence. He stood six feet three inches tall, and there was—according to the stories she would later tell about this day—something in the majesty and symmetry of his figure which made him look even taller. Cordiality shone from the depths of his blue eyes, and his gracious voice and manner soon put her at her ease.

General Washington lost no time. He drew a sheet of paper from his pocket which showed a rough design of a flag with 13 stripes—like the Grand Union Flag—and 13 stars. Spreading the paper out on the table, he asked her if she thought she could reproduce it in bunting and secure an effective arrangement of the red, white and blue.

She inspected the design for an instant and replied that she would gladly try. Then, noting the stars in the design were six-pointed, she quickly volunteered, 'I think the correct star should have five points.'

The General and his companions agreed with her, but said they felt a six-pointed star could be more easily made, and that a large number of flags might soon be required. To this Betsy responded by deftly folding a scrap of paper. Then, with a single clip of her scissors, she displayed to the astonished eyes of her visitors a perfectly symmetrical five-pointed star.

With this issue settled, other particulars were discussed and agreed upon. The flag was to be made with red stripes at top and bottom, making seven red and six white stripes. The canton was to be a blue square with thirteen white stars arranged in the form of a circle. When asked how soon she could finish the flag, Betsy replied, 'Very quickly.'

She had never before made a flag, but this did not disconcert her. It had been suggested that for guidance in the peculiar stitch and hem, she call at Robert Morris' office on the waterfront to obtain a sample of a ship's flag, and this she did. An old flag was pulled from a chest in the office. She carefully examined its make-up—its extra rows of stitching at the seams, its heavy sailcloth binding at the side with strongly sewn eyelets for attachment to staff or peak. She was told to take it with her if she wished. On her way home, she stopped at a

supply store for some bunting, and was soon hard at work on her task.

She worked far into the night in her candlelit living room, and when morning dawned, she had completed the first American Flag.

She notified Ross and Morris, who expressed complete satisfaction with the flag, and who praised her skill and promptness, telling her they might require her further assistance, and that they would let her know General Washington's opinion.

Meanwhile, the British were closing in on New York by land and sea, and General Washington had to cut short his Philadelphia visit and hurry back to command the Army. As the legend goes, she never spoke with him again, but Colonel Ross returned the next day to tell her that the design had been accepted. He also gave her some money to defray expenses, and directed her to make up a number of additional flags.

What became of that first Stars and Stripes made by Betsy Ross will never be known.

The claim that Betsy Ross helped to design and make the first American Flag is based on affidavits from some of her daughters, nieces, granddaughters and others. The statements were first made public by William J Canby, Betsy Ross' grandson, in a paper which he read before the Historical Society of Pennsylvania in 1870. These affidavits allege that, on many occasions before her death in 1836, Mrs Ross told her daughters, nieces and others the story of how she had partly designed and made the first American Flag.

Above: On 2 July 1777, The Stars and Stripes was displayed for the first time in the Navy by Captain John Paul Jones, in command of the USS *Ranger.*

On 24 April 1778, John Paul Jones, in command of the USS *Ranger*, achieved the honor of being the first officer of the American Navy to compel a British man-of-war, the HMS *Drake*, to strike her colors to the new American Flag.

Above: George Washington and members of the Continental Congress watch as the first Flag is raised at Independence Hall in Philadelphia.

Right: The Flag of the United States as adopted on 14 June 1777. In the early flags, the 13 stars were arranged in different ways, including the form of a circle, as shown. The circle was intended to signify that the Union would be without end and to symbolize equality among the states. However, there was no officially prescribed arrangement of the stars until the issuance of the President's executive order of 24 June 1912.

In later years, historians and Flag authorities frowned on the Betsy Ross story for many reasons. The journals of the Continental Congress make no mention of the meeting, and, although Washington was a voluminous letter writer and kept very detailed diaries, none of these writings mention any connection he may have had with a matter as interesting and as important as the designing and making of the first United States Flag. None of the historians of the Revolutionary War period make reference to the meeting, nor did any of the Philadelphia newspapers issued at the time chronicle any portion of the story that before the flag which Betsy Ross made was submitted to Congress it was displayed on a vessel at the wharf.

Despite the fact that the Betsy Ross story is entirely based on oral history, the likelihood of her fabricating such a story seems remote. In any event, it is certainly one of the most compelling elements of American folklore relating to Our Flag.

The Stars and Stripes

On 4 July 1776, four weeks after Betsy Ross' rendezvous with history, the Continental Congress officially declared the United States to be independent of Great Britain. Although it would be a year before the Flag was officially adopted, there is evidence that it was in use throughout the intervening months.

On June 14, 1777, the Continental Congress in Philadelphia adopted the following resolution, which established the Stars and Stripes as the official National Flag: 'Resolved, That the Flag of the United States be 13 stripes, alternate red and white; that the union be 13 stars, white in a blue field representing a new constellation.'

The wording of the resolution left much to the imagination and inclination of future makers and users of Our Flag. For example, it does not state whether the stripes should be horizontal or vertical, although it was evidently intended that they should be horizontal, as in the Grand Union or Cambridge Flag. Nor does it prescribe the number of points of the stars or their arrangement in the blue field. Neither does it indicate the proportions of the Flag and the proportions of the blue field, although all of these issues were said to have been resolved by Betsy Ross.

Even today, flag designing is really a branch of heraldry and ideally should be in accordance with its laws, both in the forms and colors introduced. Yellow is the equivalent of gold, and white of silver, and it is one of the requirements of heraldry that color should not be placed upon color nor metal upon metal. However, it is evident from the national flags of many nations that not everyone adheres to the precepts of heraldry. In regulation flags, the assemblage of colors is held to be sufficient, and anything of the nature of an inscription is rare.

The red, white and blue chosen by the colonists were, in fact, placed according to the rules of heraldry. The 13 stripes, side-by-side, are said to recall the history of the eight long, bitter years of suffering and

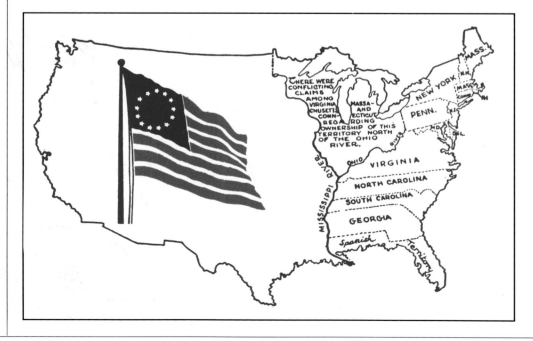

sacrifice that marked the birth of the nation, during which the 13 Colonies, side-by-side, fought for freedom. The red proclaims the courage which Americans have always shown, the courage that inspires men and women to face danger, to do what is right, to fear no one, to hesitate at nothing when honor and duty call. It was Washington who, in describing the Flag, said, 'We take the star from heaven, the red from the Mother Country, separating it by white stripes, thus showing that we have separated from her, and the white stripes shall go down to posterity representing liberty.' The blue is seen as standing for loyalty. It is the blue of the heavens, the 'true blue.' It tells the story of thousands of men and women who have been loyal to their country through suffering and hardship.

The United States Flag has seven red stripes and six white and not seven white and six red because if there were seven white stripes, the outer stripes would be white, which at a distance would not be very visible. Thus, the the outer stripes are red, which necessitates having seven red ones.

The star is an ancient symbol of Egypt, Persia and India, signifying sovereignty and dominion. However, it is not known why the founding fathers placed stars in the blue field of the Flag. It is suggested by some, though without tangible evidence, that the stars and stripes in the coat of arms of the Washington family determined the original design of Our Flag. Others, especially loyal Rhode Islanders, are quick to maintain that the stars were suggested by the 13 white stars in the blue field of their 1775 flag.

If the claim that the stars in the American Flag were suggested by the stars in Washington's coat of arms is in fact true, it means that the stars represented in Our Flag came from the bottom of the sea instead of from the sky! It seems that on the surface of the soil in the Midland shires of England, where Washington's ancestors lived, people often found small, five-pointed, star-shaped stones—fossilized crinoids, or sea lilies. Wherever found, these little star-shaped stones have always attracted attention, usually being regarded with superstition as something supernatural. Because of the superstitious awe with which they were looked upon by the common people, they quite naturally appeared upon the coats of arms of the important families the regions where they were found, as was the case with the Washington family.

The 13 stars stood, of course, for the 13 states of New Hampshire, Massachusetts, Rhode Island, Connecticut, Delaware, Maryland, Virginia, North Carolina, South Carolina, Georgia, New York, New Jersey and Pennsylvania.

Vermont joined the Union in 1791, and Kentucky (which was part of Virginia but later formed into a separate state, just as Tennessee was formed out of North Carolina) in 1792. There were, therefore, 15 states and not thirteen, and to meet these new conditions, Congress declared on 15 January 1794 that '[F]rom and after the first day of May 1795, the Flag of the United States be 15 stripes and the union be 15 stars.'

The circular format, in which the stars symbolized 'union without end' was thus abandoned after being in use for 18 years. The new Flag, with 15 stars, had them arranged in five horizontal rows of three each, those of the second and fourth rows being below the intervals between the others.

Below: Enormous American flags flapped in the breeze as Southern Pacific Railroad employees posed for a group photograph at their San Francisco headquarters on a summer day in 1902.

THE EVOLUTION OF OUR FLAG

A fter 1795, when the Flag evolved from 13 stars and stripes to 15 of both, there was little difficulty in dealing with an increase among the stars, although every additional stripe was seen to weaken the aesthetic effect. By 1818, when five other states had been brought in and the future had others in store, it became evident that the original idea of a *stripe* as well as a star for each state would simply ruin the appearance of the Flag, so on 4 April of that year, Congress decided that the number of stripes should be reduced permanently to 13, and that the union should then have 20 stars, with a new star added

for each new state admitted. This flag was first flown on the House of Representatives on 13 April 1818 and the 20 stars were arranged in the form of a large five-pointed star. However, this format was soon abandoned and the stars placed in rows.

The Star-Spangled Banner

The 15-star/15-stripe Flag was still in service when the song about that Flag, which eventually became the National Anthem, was written.

It was September 1814. England and the United States were at war again, and a powerful British fleet, carrying thousands of soldiers, had arrived in Chesapeake Bay for the purpose of destroying the large number of American privateers which had been going out from the bay to raid British shipping. The British were also intent on using the bay as a base from which a massive land force would advance northward toward Washington, DC. At the same time an army from Canada was to force its way southward through the Valley of the Hud-

son. The plan, as had been the case during the revolution, was to split the country in two along the line of the Hudson, the Delaware and the Chesapeake. It was perceived that the United States was to be invaded and subjugated again.

Five thousand British troops, landing at a point on the Patuxent River, a tributary of Chesapeake Bay 20 miles from Washington, advanced on the city, and, after forcing President Madison, his Cabinet and other officials to flee, they burned the Capitol and the White House, and ransacked other public buildings. The enemy forces then returned to their ships and sailed for Baltimore, the next point of their attack.

British troops were landed at North

Facing page: 'By the dawn's early light' on 14 September 1814, Francis Scott Key completed *The Star-Spangled Banner*, the song that would become the National Anthem. The specific flag which Key observed that morning at Fort McHenry, Maryland, is now preserved at the Smithsonian Institution in Washington, DC. Note that it has both 15 stars and 15 stripes.

Point, a few miles from Baltimore, and the fleet continued on, preparing for action off Fort McHenry, which stood like a forbidding sentinel in the defense of Baltimore.

When informed that nearly all the troops defending Baltimore were of the militia, General Ross, commander of the British land forces, flushed with the victory of Washington, boastfully said, 'I will take Baltimore if it rains militia.' When asked at breakfast on the morning of 13 September whether supper should be prepared for him at the same place, he answered, voicing the sentiment of his army, 'I will have supper in Baltimore or in hell.' At another time he had boastfully remarked, 'I will make my winter headquarters in Baltimore and subjugate the whole coast.'

A few hours after the land attack was launched, the fleet began to bombard Fort McHenry, with every one of the 16 British ships concentrating its fire on the low-lying fortification, whose flagpole was flying the 15-star Flag.

Shells rained on the small Fort and its defenders. One of the American guns was shot off its carriage, but a number of men put it up again. Several of the enemy's ships moved nearer to fire on the crowd, but the Yanks raked them so fiercely, they promptly withdrew.

Meanwhile, detained on a small vessel, the *Minden*, among the British ships, was a lawyer from Georgetown named Francis Scott Key, who had only a few days before seen the capital looted. As an official envoy, he had gone to see the British admiral when the fleet was in the Patuxent River, regarding the release of an aged American doctor, an intimate friend, who was being held prisoner. Fearing that he

might reveal information about the plans being made to advance on Baltimore, Key was detained aboard a British ship, to be held until after the bombardment was completed.

Watching the battle continue as night fell, Key withdrew an envelope from his pocket and began jotting down notes: 'And the rocket's red glare, the bomb bursting in air,' he wrote, 'gave proof through the night that Our Flag was still there!'

Frustrated by the stubborn resistance of the Americans, the British decided to close in, and, under cover of darkness, to land several hundred hand-picked men to attack the garrison from the rear. However, as their landing boats attempted to steal past the fortifications, they were discovered and driven back to their ships in confusion.

At midnight, there was a lull in the battle, and the British learned that the land attack during the day had failed and that General Ross had been killed. In desperation, the fleet moved nearer and redoubled its fire. The fort answered, gun for gun. In the wee hours of the morning, the bombardment finally ceased, and in the silence and darkness, Francis Scott Key anxiously wondered if the Flag was still intact. At last, at daybreak, his eager eyes peered through the morning mist, straining to see the low fort. Again, he took out his pencil and by the first light of the morning he wrote:

O, say can you see, by the dawn's early
    light,
What so proudly we hail'd at the
    twilight's last gleaming,
Whose broad stripes and bright stars
    through the perilous fight,
O'er the ramparts we watched, were so
    gallantly streaming?

Key wondered at first whether the flag he saw was the stars and stripes or the British Union Jack. The mist was still clearing, and the banner still half concealed:

What is that which the breeze, o'er the
    towering steep,
As it fitfully blows, half conceals, half
    discloses?

Finally, able to see clearly that the Flag 'catches the gleam of the morning's first beam,' Key wrote:

'Tis the star-spangled banner—O long
    may it wave
O'er the land of the free and the home
    of the brave!

Below: The state of Vermont was admitted into the Union in 1791 and Kentucky in 1792. The representatives of these two states in Congress wanted their states recognized in the flag, so on 13 January 1794, Congress enacted the following law: 'That from and after the first day of May, 1795, the flag of the United States be 15 stripes, alternate red and white; and that the union be 15 stars, white, in a blue field.'

In 1818, when the stars in the flag were increased to 20, following the admission of Tennessee (1796), Ohio (1802), Louisiana (1812), Indiana (1816) and Mississippi (1817). The number of stripes was in turn reduced to 13.

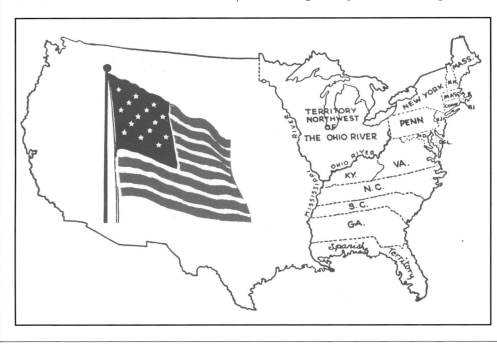

Key finished the poem on his way back to the shore that morning, and after he arrived at a hotel in Baltimore, he made a copy of the four verses, which he took to Judge Joseph H Nicholson the following morning to ask him what he thought of it. The judge was so pleased with the poem, he sent it to a printer and directed that copies be struck off in handbill form.

It was set in type by Samuel Sands, an apprentice in the office of the *Baltimore American*, and handbills were distributed throughout the city. An examination of one of these handbills is interesting, for the poem was entitled *Defense of Fort M'Henry*. Above the poem were the words 'Tune— *Anacreon in Heaven*.' This tune was a popular air of the time, and it is believed that Key had this song in mind when he wrote his poem. The involved meter and peculiar form of his poem substantiate this. However, the name of the author of the poem was omitted.

Due to the fact that printing of newspapers in Baltimore was suspended from 10 September to 20 September, the poem did not appear in a newspaper until 20 September, when the *Baltimore Patriot* printed it, set up in the same manner as the handbills. On 21 September, the *Baltimore American* printed it as well.

Much confusion exists concerning the 'correct' wording and punctuation of *The Star-Spangled Banner*, which came to be known by this title through popular usage. The reason the confusion exists is that there seems to have been, not counting the original draft, at least five copies of the verses in Key's own handwriting, in which Key himself made changes in the original wording.

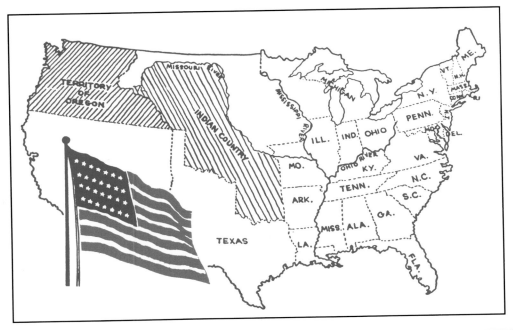

Above: The HMS *Guerriere*, its Union Jack trailing in the ship's wake, has been boarded by the men of the USS *Constitution* who proudly fly the 13-star Flag from, not one, but three masts.

Left: Following the admission into the Union of Mississippi in 1817, Illinois, Alabama, Maine, Missouri, Arkansas, Michigan, Florida and Texas were admitted during the period ending 13 May 1846. Meanwhile the number of stripes was permanently established at 13.

When the war was declared against Mexico on that day, there were 28 stars in the Flag, arranged in four rows of seven each. The next time that all the rows would have seven stars would be in 1959, when the 49-star Flag—with seven rows of seven—was adopted.

Above: The battle flag belonging to the 8th Pennsylvania Infantry, circa 1864, as photographed by Matthew Brady.

From the beginning of the Mexican War to 1861, when the Civil War began, six more states—Iowa, Wisconsin, California, Minnesota, Oregon and Kansas—were admitted into the Union. The stars in the Flag then numbered 34 and were arranged in five horizontal rows, the first and second rows having seven stars each, the third row, six, and the fourth and fifth rows, seven stars each.

In the first verse, the third line, 'broad stripes and bright stars' was also written 'bright stars and broad stripes.' In this same verse the word 'perilous' was also written as 'clouds of the,' while in the fifth line 'bomb' was also written 'bombs.' In the second verse, the most interesting difference occurs in the fourth line where the word 'half,' used twice, was also written 'now' twice. In the third verse, first line, the phrase 'is that band who' was also written 'are the foes that,' 'are the foes who,' 'that host that' and 'the foe that.'

Also in this same line, the word 'vauntingly' was also written 'sweepingly.' In the fourth verse, the first word of the first line, 'O' was also written 'and,' and the word 'freemen' was also written 'foemen.' In the seventh line, the wording 'in triumph shall' was also written 'O long may it.'

These various versions were copied by different compilers, and in the course of time, verbal changes, some intentional and some in error, crept in, so the text has become quite unsettled.

The third stanza, beginning with 'And where is that band who so vauntingly swore' is quite often omitted, and it may be said this had often been done because the verse is expressive of rather bitter sentiment against the British.

Such sentiment was certainly natural and logical in 1814, but became rather unnatural and illogical in later years after the two nations formed a close alliance.

It was not for over a century, however, that the song was officially adopted as the National Anthem. An act of Congress, approved 3 March 1931 by President Herbert Hoover, made *The Star-Spangled Banner* our National Anthem: 'Be it enacted by the Senate and House of Representatives of the United States of America in Congress assembled, That the composition consisting of the words and music known as the *The Star-Spangled Banner* is designated the National Anthem of the United States of America.' It is worthy to note that in this act, the 'T' in 'The' is capitalized and 'Star-Spangled' is hyphenated.

In view of the fact that, as shown above, there are several different versions of both text and music of *The Star-Spangled Banner*, our National Anthem would have been much more complete if the act of Congress had given the text and music of the version adopted as the National Anthem.

Inspired to heights he had never before reached, Francis Scott Key, writing on one small envelope he had found in his pocket, poured out of his soul the inspiring words of *The Star-Spangled Banner*. From that terrible night at Fort McHenry in 1814—to 1991, when Whitney Houston's stirring rendition at the Super Bowl became number one on the pop charts—this song has gone forth to sing itself into the hearts of each new generation of Americans.

The Constellation Grows

After the War of 1812 concluded with Andrew Jackson's rout of British forces in the Battle of New Orleans, the United States—and the constellation of stars upon the field of blue—continued to grow. Through 1818, when the Flag Law was passed, three additional states were admitted into the Union: Louisiana in 1812, Indiana in 1816 and Mississippi in 1817. In order to give these five states representation in the flag, Congress on 4 April 1818 enacted the following law:

Section 1. That from and after the fourth day of July next, the Flag of the United States be 13 horizontal stripes, alternate red and white; that the Union have 20 stars, white on a blue field.

Section 2. That on the admission of every state into the Union, one star be added to the Union of the Flag; and that such addition shall take effect on the Fourth of July next succeeding admission.

After the admission of Mississippi in 1817, Illinois, Alabama, Maine, Missouri, Arkansas, Michigan, Florida and Texas were admitted during the period ending 13 May 1846, so that when the war was on that day declared against Mexico, there were 28 stars in the Flag, arranged in four rows of seven each.

Six more states—Iowa, Wisconsin, California, Minnesota, Oregon and Kansas—were admitted into the Union from the beginning of the Mexican War to 1861. When the Civil War started, the stars in Our Flag numbered 34, arranged in five horizontal rows, with the first and second rows having seven stars each, the third row six and the fourth and fifth rows, seven stars each.

It is worthy to note that these states—all northern states were admitted as 'free' states to give the anti-slavery members in Congress a decisive edge. It did little good, and, in April 1861, the United States found itself torn apart by the Civil War.

THE EVOLUTION OF OUR FLAG

The Stars and Bars

In 1861, when the States of the Confederacy declared their independence from the United States, they set about adopting a single national flag for the Confederate States of America. A special committee was appointed to consider the matter, and upon presenting their report, the chairman of this committee said: 'A flag should be simple, readily made and capable of being made up in bunting. It should be different from the flag of any other country, place or people. It should be significant. It should be readily distinguishable at a distance. The colors should be well contrasted and durable. And lastly, and not the least important point, it should be effective and handsome. The committee humbly thinks that the flag which they submit combines these requirements. It is very easy to make. It is entirely different from any other national flag. The three colors of which it is composed—red, white and blue—are the true republican colors. They are emblematic of the three great virtues—valor, purity and truth. Naval men assure us that it can be recognized at a great distance. The colors contrast admirably, and are lasting. In effect and appearance, it must speak for itself.'

As the United States Flag had 13 horizontal *stripes*, The Stars and Bars had three horizontal *bars* of red, white, red, with a large blue canton on which there was a circle of seven white stars, representing the original seven states of the Confederacy. This circular arrangement, adopted with the old idea of all states alike—as if they each had a *particular* star—was phased out when the number of Confederate States increased to 11. This flag, known as either The Stars and Bars *or* The Southern Cross, was not a rendition of the Southern Cross constellation, as we see in the Australian Flag, but rather, a blue St Andrew's Cross edged with white on a red field with stars along the arms. First flown at the Battle of Manassas in July 1861, this flag became the official Confederate *battle* flag for the rest of the war, although it was never the official *national* flag.

The difficulty with this flag was to arrange the 11 stars in a satisfactory way, and in the most successful version this was evaded by boldly inserting 13 in the anticipation that two other states would join the Confederacy. Another objection was raised to the flag, suggesting that—like the Cross of St George—it could not be used as a signal of distress, as there was no upside or downside to it. To satisfy this argument, it was used as a canton in the upper left hand corner of a white flag, which was in turn decried as being too much like a truce flag. It was therefore decided to add a broad, vertical band of red to the end of the white, and this, the fourth flag of the Confederacy, was adopted on 4 February 1865.

It was short-lived, however, as the Confederacy died at Appomattox Court House on 9 April 1865, and with it The Stars and Bars. The motif was, however, later revived for inclusion in the Mississippi state flag.

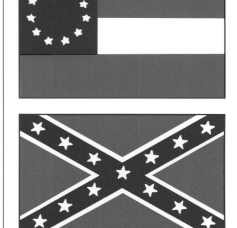

Above: The Stars and Bars (*top*) was the official national flag of the Confederate States of America from 1861 to 1865, but the Confederate battle flag (*bottom*)is the most often remembered flag of the Confederacy.

Below: The Confederate ironclad *Merrimac,* proudly flying the Stars and Bars in its famous 1862 battle with the Union ironclad USS *Monitor.*

Old Glory

It was on 17 March 1824 in Salem, Massachusetts that a 21-year-old, would-be sailor named William Driver was presented by his mother and a group of friends with a beautiful American Flag they had made for him.

'I name her "Old Glory,"' he said in response to their greetings—and thus it was that the name 'Old Glory' entered the American lexicon. From that day on, 'Old Glory' accompanied Driver whenever he went to sea—twice around the world, once around Australia and several other cruises.

In 1837, when Captain Driver quit the sea and settled in Nashville, Tennessee, 'Old Glory' accompanied him. On occasions such as Washington's birthday, the Fourth of July and St Patrick's Day (also Driver's birthday), 'Old Glory' could be seen gracefully waving from a rope extending from the Captain's house to a tree across the street.

However, in 1861, when Tennessee seceded from the Union and hostilities began, 'Old Glory' mysteriously vanished.

On the morning of 25 February 1862, Union soldiers entered Nashville and took possession of the city. On that morning Driver, accompanied by Captain Thatcher of the Sixth Ohio Regiment and several soldiers, came home, and, calling his daughter Mary Jane, asked her to help him rip a bed cover the was holding. As the comforter was ripped apart, there was 'Old Glory'! The flag had been sewn between the folds of the cover for safe-keeping when Tennessee had seceded and American Flags became objects of attack in the city.

At the sight of 'Old Glory,' the soldiers cheered, and then helped to fold the flag, which Captain Driver took in his arms as the party left for the State House. Shortly thereafter, the Captain climbed to the dome of the building and raised 'Old Glory' over the capitol, exclaiming, 'Thank God! I lived to raise "Old Glory" on the dome of the capitol of Tennessee. I am now ready to die and go to my forefathers.'

Below: A Union officer carries the 34-star American Flag in this stirring but somewhat fanciful rendering of the Federal triumph at Petersburg.

The Great Westward Expansion

After the Civil War, the attention of the nation was turned to settling the vast area between the Missouri River and the Pacific coastal states, which was then known as the 'Wild West.' With this westward expansion came the addition of new states, and as former territories achieved statehood, new stars appeared on the flag.

Nebraska, in 1867, was the first to be added on the heels of the war, and Colorado joined during the nation's centennial year in August 1876.

A major milestone in the history of Our Flag came in 1889, when more stars were added in a single year than at any time since the adoption of the original 13-star Flag in 1777.

The four states—Montana, Washington and the two Dakotas—that joined in November 1889 were followed by Idaho and Wyoming in July 1890. Together they constituted an addition to the nation into which the area of the original 13 could be fitted many times over. Utah, in 1896, was the last state to join the Union in the nineteenth century.

When the twentieth century began, the area of the contiguous United States contained 45 states and four territories. How then did 45 plus four come to equal the 48 that characterized the United States for most of the century?

It happened that the Indian Territory, created just north of Texas in 1837 for the Cherokee, Creek, Seminole, Choctaw and Chickasaw Nations had been split in two in 1891 for the creation of the Oklahoma Territory. In fact, both territories still existed in 1907, although the Indian Territory had been greatly truncated.

In November 1907, however, the Indian Territory was officially dissolved and merged into Oklahoma as the latter achieved statehood, adding a 46th star to the Flag. New Mexico and Arizona joined on 6 January and 14 February 1912, respectively, and the contiguous United States, with its 48-star flag, was complete.

Below: Jerry Pordilla, a member of the Kiowa tribe, in his grandfather's nineteenth-century costume.

Flag Day

The Fourth of July was traditionally celebrated as America's national birthday, but the idea of an annual day specifically celebrating the Flag seems to have first originated in 1885. BJ Cigrand, a schoolteacher, arranged for the pupils in the Fredonia, Wisconsin Public School, District 6, to observe 14 June (the 108th anniversary of the official adoption of The Stars and Stripes) as 'Flag Birthday.' In numerous magazine and newspaper articles and public addresses over the following years, Cigrand continued to enthusiastically advocate the observance of 14 June as 'Flag Birthday,' or 'Flag Day.'

On 14 June 1889, George Balch, a kindergarten teacher in New York City, planned appropriate ceremonies for the children of his school, and his idea of observing Flag Day was later adopted by the State Board of Education of New York. On 14 June 1891, the Betsy Ross House in Philadelphia held a Flag Day celebration, and on 14 June of the following year, the New York Society of the Sons of the Revolution, celebrated Flag Day.

Following the suggestion of Colonel J Granville Leach (at the time historian of the Pennsylvania Society of Sons of the Revolution), the Pennsylvania Society of Colonial Dames of America on 25 April 1893 adopted a resolution requesting the mayor of Philadelphia and all others in authority and all private citizens to display the Flag on 14 June. Leach went on to recommend that thereafter the day be known as 'Flag Day,' and on that day, school children be assembled for appropriate exercises, with each child being given a small Flag.

Below: Two 48-star Flags and a poster of Woodrow Wilson for President are the backdrop in this photo showing WA McGirt, President of New Hanover Food Conservation Commission. President Wilson established the 14th day of June as the nation's Flag Day.

Two weeks later on 8 May, the Board of Managers of the Pennsylvania Society of Sons of the Revolution unanimously endorsed the action of the Pennsylvania Society of Colonial Dames. As a result of the resolution, Dr Edward Brooks, then Superintendent of Public Schools of Philadelphia, directed that Flag Day exercises be held on 14 June 1893 in Independence Square. School children were assembled, each carrying a small Flag, and patriotic songs were sung and addresses delivered.

In 1894, the governor of New York directed that on 14 June the Flag be displayed on all public buildings. With BJ Cigrand and Leroy Van Horn as the moving spirits, the Illinois organization, known as the American Flag Day Association, was organized for the purpose of promoting the holding of Flag Day exercises. On 14 June 1894, under the auspices of this association, the first general public school children's celebration of Flag Day in Chicago was held in Douglas, Garfield, Humboldt, Lincoln and Washington Parks, with more than 300,000 children participating.

Inspired by these three decades of state and local celebrations, Flag Day was officially established by the Proclamation of President Woodrow Wilson on 30 May 1916:

'My fellow countrymen: Many circumstances have recently conspired to turn our thoughts to a critical examination of the conditions of our national life, of the influences which have seemed to threatened to divide us in interest and sympathy, of forces within and forces without that seemed likely to draw us away from the happy traditions of united purpose and action of which we have been so proud. It has, therefore, seemed to me fitting that I should call your attention to the approach of the anniversary of the day upon which

Below: American troops cheering and displaying the Stars and Stripes at a Russian port as they await the tender that will take them home after the 1918 deployment of US Army forces to Russia.

the Flag of the United States was adopted by the Congress as the emblem of the Union, and to suggest to you that it should this year and in the years to come be given special significance as a day of renewal and reminder, a day upon which we should direct our minds with a special desire of renewal to thoughts of the ideals and principles of which we have sought to make our great government the embodiment.

'I therefore suggest and request that throughout the nation, and, if possible, in every community, the 14th day of June be observed as Flag Day, with special patriotic exercises, at which means shall be taken to give significant expression to our thoughtful love of America, our comprehension of the great mission of liberty and justice to which we have devoted ourselves as a people, our pride in our history and our enthusiasm for the political program of the nation, our determination to make it greater and purer with each generation, and our resolution to demonstrate to all the world its vital union in sentiment and purpose, accepting only those as true compatriots who feel as we do the compulsion of this supreme allegiance. Let us on that day rededicate ourselves to the nation, "one and inseparable," from which every thought that is not worthy of our fathers' first vows in independence, liberty and right shall be excluded and in which we shall stand, with united hearts, for an America which no man can corrupt, no influence draw away from its ideals, no force divide against itself—a nation signally distinguished among all the nations of mankind for its clear, individual conception alike of its duties and its privileges, its obligations and its rights.'

The Wilson proclamation establishing Flag Day was the culmination of a quarter century of separate and unconnected efforts by individuals and organizations in various parts of the country in the interest of the observance of 14 June as Flag Day. This proclamation gave authoritative, nationwide expression to the sentiment which, for years, had been accumulating in favor of a general observance of Flag Day.

On 7 June 1922, President Calvin Coolidge issued to the American people the following statement regarding the Flag:

'My fellow Americans: Flag Day on 14 June will mark the 150th anniversary of the adoption by Congress of The Stars and Stripes as the emblem of our nation. It is fitting that we should recall all that Our Flag means, what it represents to our citizens and to the nations of the Earth.

'There should be no more appropriate time to give thanks for the blessings that have descended upon our people in this century and a half, and to rededicate ourselves to the high principles for which our Ensign stands. Liberty and union, freedom of thought and speech under the rule of reason and righteousness as expressed in our constitution and laws, the protection of life and property, the continuation of justice in our domestic and foreign relations—these are among the high ideals of which Our Flag is the visible symbol.

'It will be futile merely to show outward respect of our National Emblem if we do not cherish in our hearts an unquenchable love of, and devotion to, the unseen which it represents.

'To the end that we may direct our attention to these things, I suggest that Flag Day be observed in the display of The Stars and Stripes in public places and upon public and private buildings and by patriotic exercises in our schools and community centers throughout the land.'

Below: US Army troops march down the streets of Washington, DC on 6 August 1991 during the Operation *Desert Storm* national victory celebration parade. In accordance with the Flag Code, Our Flag is displayed in the place of superior prominence—to the right of all other flags.

Facing page: Sailors from Pelham Bay Naval Training Station march down Fifth Avenue in 1918 during the Fourth Liberty Loan Parade in New York City. While the colors are not being carried, patriotic citizens have displayed the Flag from flagpoles high above the crowds.

Young America and Our Flag. Two Girl Scouts (*above*) stand at attention, while Brownies and Daisy Girl Scouts (*below*) cover their hearts for the Pledge of Allegiance. A Cub Scout (*facing page*) executes a snappy salute as the Flag passes by.

Flag Week, the week beginning 8 June and ending on Flag Day on 14 June each year, which was inaugurated in 1939 by The United States Flag Association, was originated by the President General of the Association, Colonel James A Moss, US Army, Retired. The purpose of Flag Week was to 'stimulate and promote national unity (a united citizenship free from class hatred and working together in all matters affecting the welfare of the nation), patriotic cooperation (between capital, labor and government) and tolerance (in racial, religious and other matters).'

The Pledge of Allegiance

The original Pledge to the Flag was written in 1892 at the offices of the Perry Mason Company of Boston, publishers of the magazine *The Youth's Companion*, where it was published in the 8 September issue. As originally written, it read: 'I Pledge allegiance to my Flag and to the republic for which it stands; one nation indivisible, with liberty and justice for all.'

It was first officially used during the National Public Schools Celebration of 21 October 1892, which took place at the same time as the opening of the World's Columbian Exposition in Chicago. On that occasion, it was repeated by millions of public school children throughout the United States.

At the First National Flag Conference held in Washington on 14-15 June 1923, the words 'the Flag of the United States' were substituted for 'my Flag,' making the Pledge read: 'I pledge allegiance to the Flag of the United States and to the Republic for which it stands; one nation indivisible, with liberty and justice for all.'

This change was made on the grounds that some foreign-born children and others born in this country of foreign parentage, when rendering the Pledge, had in mind the flag of their native land, or that of their parents, when they said 'my Flag.'

The Second National Flag conference held in Washington on Flag Day, 1924, added, for the sake of greater definition,

Opposite: On 23 February 1945, during World War II, Associated Press photographer Joe Rosenthal took the most famous photograph of an American Flag raising ever, as Marines hoisted The Stars and Stripes atop Mount Suribachi on Iwo Jima.

Below: The arrangement of the stars in the 48-star Flag is clearly visible in this view of the flagpole which the Marines had anchored in the boulders and shell fragments atop Iwo Jima's Mount Suribachi in February 1945.

the words 'of America' after 'Flag of the United States,' so that the Pledge now read: 'I pledge allegiance to the Flag of the United States of America and to the republic for which it stands; one nation indivisible, with liberty and justice for all.' In 1954, Congress added to the Pledge the phrase 'under God' after 'nation.'

Meanwhile, the question of authorship of the Pledge came into dispute. It seems that at the time the Pledge was written, both Francis Bellamy of Rome, New York, and James Upham of Malden, Massachusetts, were associated with *The Youth's Companion*, and the families of each claimed the authorship of the original Pledge to the Flag.

In 1939, to determine, in the interest of historical accuracy and certainty, the authorship of the original Pledge, The United States Flag Association appointed a committee consisting of Charles C Tansill, professor of American history at Fordham

Above: The American Flag was raised for the first time on another body in the Solar System when Neil Armstrong and Edwin Aldrin planted Old Glory in the Sea of Tranquillity on the Moon on 20 July 1969.

Below: Astronaut John Young of Apollo 16 paused to salute the fifth American Flag to be planted on lunar soil.

Facing page: With the blue Earth visible a quarter million miles away, Astronaut Harrison Schmitt of Apollo 17 planted this Flag on the lunar surface in December 1972. Apollo 17's Flag was the sixth American Flag placed on the Moon.

University; W Reed West, professor of political science, George Washington University; and Bernard Mayo, professor of American History, Georgetown University. After carefully and impartially weighing all evidence submitted by the two contending families, the committee unanimously decided that Bellamy deserved the distinctive honor of being the author of the original Pledge to the Flag. Their report was submitted to, and approved by, the national headquarters of The United States Flag Association on 18 May 1939.

Today, questions about the Pledge of Allegiance usually involve practices and requirements of local and state statues mandating participation in the recitation of the Pledge in some manner (flag salute and pledge, standing quietly, standing at attention) in schools. However, provisions involving compulsory participation in Pledge activities are usually attacked as violations of the free speech clause of the First Amendment or the free exercise of religion clause. In 1943, in fact, the Supreme Court held that a state-required compulsory flag salute/Pledge of Allegiance violated the First Amendment right of members of the Jehovah's Witnesses religious group.

Two More Make Fifty

By the end of the 1950s, the contiguous 48 states had been a nation for nearly half a century, but there was a growing statehood movement in two of the non-contiguous United States territories. Both Alaska—which was purchased from the Russian Empire in 1867—and Hawaii—which was annexed in 1898 at the urging of its citizens—now wanted to become states. There was a good deal of debate over whether to admit noncontiguous areas, but this issue seemed to be the only major stumbling block to statehood for the two territories. This was soon swept aside, and the voluminous paperwork necessary to effect the transformation began to make its way through the United States Congress and the respective state legislatures.

By the end of 1958, Alaska was ready, and on 3 January 1959, President Dwight Eisenhower officially proclaimed it the 49th State, in time for the new state's two senators and one congressman to take their seats in the 86th Congress on 6 Janu-

ary. The 49-star American Flag, with seven rows of seven stars, was unveiled in January and officially adopted on 4 July 1959. It was the shortest-lived American Flag in 70 years, for only six weeks later, on 21 August, President Eisenhower unveiled the 50-star flag.

Congress had passed the act approving Hawaii's admission on 12 March 1959, and Hawaii's voters had approved the Statehood Act on 27 June 1959, but the 50-star Flag, which debuted on 21 August, was not to be officially adopted for nearly a year. Thus, the 49-star 'Alaska' Flag remained the nation's official Flag until 4 July 1960—the 184th anniversary of the signing of the Declaration of Independence—when the Flag whose blue canton contained nine alternating rows of six and five stars, was flown for the first time. At one minute past midnight, it was raised at Fort McHenry, Maryland, the same place where the Flag immortalized by Francis Scott Key had survived through the terrible night of 13-14 September 1814. The raising of the Flag at Fort McHenry—which officially became a National Monument at the same moment—was followed by flag raisings throughout Hawaii at 12:01 am Hawaiian time five hours later.

At President Eisenhower's direction, the first official 50-star Flag was delivered from Fort McHenry to Independence Hall in Philadelphia, where, on the afternoon of 4 July, it was raised by a Marine Corps color guard in colonial uniforms. Following a two- hour ceremony, it was lowered and presented to Senator Hiram Fong (R-Hawaii), who placed the it in a box made from the wood of an elm that had stood in Independence Square in 1776. The box was placed in the state archives of Hawaii in Honolulu on the following day.

Left: Our Flag is displayed on an enormous video screen as the United States Olympic Team enters the Los Angeles Coliseum for the XXIIId Olympiad in 1984. In 1932, the 48-star American Flag flew over the Olympic Games in this same stadium.

Below: The 50-star American Flag.

Above: All American ships and aircraft sailing and flying beyond our shores carry the American Flag. The Space Shuttle is clearly no exception.

Right: Workmen apply the finishing touches to a Flag on the wing of a Space Shuttle Orbiter. Another flag will next be painted to the left of the words 'United States.'

Below: Cheering spectators wave American Flags to show their support of the troops during the *Desert Storm* national victory celebration parade in August 1991.

The Future of Our Flag

Since the admission of Alaska and Hawaii, there has been considerable speculation as to what would be the 51st state. The strongest lobby seems to be that promoting the District of Columbia for statehood, and thus it is the most probable candidate.

Nantucket has attempted to secede from Massachusetts, and from time to time there is talk of the boroughs of New York City—together with some of its suburbs in New Jersey and Connecticut—becoming a separate state.

When he was leaving office in 1977, President Gerald Ford formally proposed statehood for the Commonwealth of Puerto Rico, but the Puerto Ricans themselves seem to be less keen on the idea than the people of Guam, who would like to see their territory become a state. The United States also has eight non-self-governing territories in the Pacific and Caribbean, as well as the trusteeship of several island groups in Micronesia, but these are unlikely candidates.

Within the contiguous 48 states, the Upper Peninsula of Michigan might be a possible candidate, and the differences between northern and southern California and their people are so pronounced as to suggest that division of the Golden State might solve numerous disagreements.

If all these possible 51st state candidates did, in fact, become states, the United States Flag could easily find itself not with 51, but as many as 67 stars.

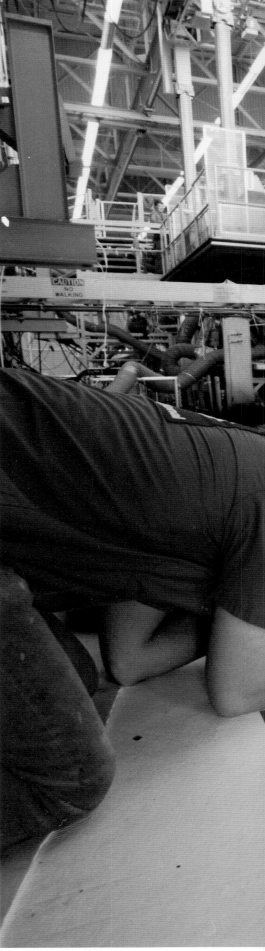

THE USE AND DISPLAY OF OUR FLAG

Facing page: When it is displayed vertically against a wall, Our Flag should have the field of stars uppermost and to the left of the viewer (the Flag's own right). If a second flag is displayed, it should be to the viewer's right.

In the case of President Reagan's inauguration in 1981, the 'second flag' was the 13-star Flag, displayed to make reference to the history of our nation—and Our Flag.

All of the states, at one time or another, have enacted laws relating to the United States Flag. Whereas the Federal Flag Code does not provide penalties for certain conduct or may not govern certain practices, state laws often do. At the national level, the Federal Flag Code (Title 36, US Code, paragraphs 170-178) provides uniform guidelines for the display of, and respect shown to, Our Flag, and conduct during playing of the National Anthem and the Pledge of Allegiance to the Flag. The Code is designed 'for the use of such civilian groups or organizations as may not be required to conform with regula-

tions promulgated by one or more executive departments' of the federal government, such as the armed forces. The Flag Code does not prescribe any penalties for non-compliance nor does it include enforcement provisions. Rather, it functions as a guide to be *voluntarily* followed by civilians and civilian groups.

While the Code empowers the President of the United States to alter, modify, repeal or prescribe additional rules regarding the Flag, no federal agency has the authority to issue 'official' rulings legally binding on civilians or civilian groups. Consequently, different interpretations of various provisions of the Code may continue to be made. The Flag Code may be fairly tested: 'No disrespect should be shown to the Flag

of the United States of America.' Therefore, actions not specifically included in the Code may be deemed acceptable as long as proper respect is shown.

In addition to the Flag Code, a separate provision contained in the Federal Criminal Code (Title 18 of the United States Code) established criminal penalties for certain treatment of Our Flag. Prior to 1989, this provision provided criminal penalties for certain acts of desecration to Our Flag. In response to the Supreme Court decision in *Texas v Johnson* on 21 June 1989, which held that anti-desecration statutes are unconstitutional if aimed at suppressing one type of expression, Congress amended the statute to provide criminal penalties for certain acts which

violate the physical integrity of the Flag.

The Flag Protection Act of 1989 (Public Law 101-131) on 28 October 1989 imposed a fine and/or up to one year in prison for knowingly mutilating, defacing, physically defiling, maintaining on the floor or trampling upon any Flag of the United States.

However, the Flag Protection Act of 1989 was struck down by the Supreme Court decision *United States v Eichman*, decided on 11 June 1990, leading to the proposal of a constitutional amendment to protect Our Flag. Ten days later, on 21 June, the House of Representatives took up the issue, voting 254 to 177 in favor of the amendment. This was 34 votes short of the two-thirds majority necessary to pass a constitutional amendment.

A poll conducted by *Newsweek* magazine and the Gallup organization found, however, that 71 percent of the people in the United States supported a constitutional amendment to protect Our Flag.

The Flag Code

The Flag Code, which is generally followed but not legally compulsory contains the following provisions:

Conduct During the Playing of the National Anthem

During rendition of the National Anthem when the flag is displayed, all present, except those in uniform, should stand at attention facing Our Flag with the right hand over the heart. Men not in uniform should remove their hats with their right hand and hold them at the left shoulder, the hand being over the heart. Persons in uniform should render the military salute at the first note of the anthem and retain this position until the last note. When Our Flag is not displayed, those present should face toward the music and act in the same manner they would if Our Flag were displayed there.

Pledge of Allegiance to the Flag

The Pledge of Allegiance to the Flag, 'I pledge allegiance to the Flag of the United States of America, and to the republic for

Below: In this photograph, our National Anthem is about to be played. Military personnel are saluting and civilians are covering their hearts with their right hands. The four buglers in the foreground will not salute, but they will participate in the playing of our National Anthem.

Facing page: When it is carried with other flags, the American Flag—here being carried by cadets at West Point—should always be on the right.

Above: When displayed with state flags (such as Wisconsin's as seen here), the American Flag is always to the right as viewed from the Flag's position or on the viewer's left.

which it stands, one nation under God, indivisible, with liberty and justice for all,' should be rendered by standing at attention facing Our Flag, with the right hand over the heart. When not in uniform, men should remove their headdress with their right hand and hold it at the left shoulder, the hand being over the heart. Persons in uniform should remain silent, face Our Flag and render the military salute.

Display and Use of Flag by Civilians

The following codification of existing rules and customs pertaining to the display and use of the Flag of the United States of America is established for the use of such civilians or civilian groups or organizations as may not be required to conform with the regulations promulgated by one or more executive departments of the government of the United States.

Time and Occasions for Display

(a) Display on buildings and stationary flagstaffs in open; night display:
It is the universal custom to display Our Flag only from sunrise to sunset on buildings and on stationary flagstaffs in the open. However, when a patriotic effect is desired, Our Flag may be displayed 24 hours a day, if

properly illuminated during the hours of darkness.

(b) Manner of hoisting:
Our Flag should be hoisted briskly and lowered ceremoniously.

(c) Inclement weather:
Our Flag should not be displayed on days when the weather is inclement, except when an all-weather flag is displayed.

(d) Particular days of display:
Our Flag should be displayed on all days, especially on 1 January (New Year's Day), 20 January (Inauguration Day), 12 February (Lincoln's Birthday), Washington's Birthday (the third Monday in February), Easter Sunday (variable); Mother's Day (the second Sunday in May), Armed Forces Day (the third Saturday in May), Memorial Day (half-staff until noon) the last Monday in May, 14 June (14 June), 4 July (Independence Day), Labor Day (the first Monday in September), 17 September (Constitution Day), Columbus Day (the second Monday in October), 27 October (Navy Day), 11 November (Veterans Day), Thanksgiving Day (the fourth Thursday in November), 25 December (Christmas Day), and such other days as may be proclaimed by the President of the United States, as well as the birthdays of states (dates of admission), and on state holidays.

(e) Display on or near administration building of public institutions:
Our Flag should be displayed daily on or near the main administration building of every public institution.

(f) Display in or near polling places:
Our Flag should be displayed in or near every polling place on election days.

(g) Display in or near schoolhouses:
Our Flag should be displayed during school days in or near every schoolhouse.

There are eight sites in the United States where Our Flag is flown day and night under specific legal authority: Fort McHenry National Monument, Baltimore, Maryland (Presidential Proclamation 2795, 2 July 1948); Flag House Square, Baltimore, Maryland (Act of 26 March 1954); United States Marine Corps Iwo Jima Memorial at Arlington, Virginia (Presidential Proclamation 3418, 12 June 1961); Lexington, Massachusetts (Public Law 89-355, 8 November 1965); the White House (Presidential Proclamation 4000, 4 September

1970); the Washington Monument (Presidential Proclamation 4064, 10 July 1971); United States Customs ports of entry (Presidential Proclamation 4131, 9 May 1972); and Valley Forge State Park, Pennsylvania (Public Law 94-53, 4 July 1975).

As a matter of custom, and without specific statutory or official authorization, Our Flag is flown at night at many other sites, including the United States Capitol, so it would seem that the display of Our Flag in a respectful manner with appropriate lighting does not violate the spirit of the Flag Code, since the dignity accorded to Our Flag is preserved by lighting that prevents its being enveloped in darkness.

The language of this section reflects the now popular use of Flags made of synthetic fabrics that can withstand unfavorable weather conditions. Thus, it is no longer considered disrespectful to fly such a Flag even during prolonged periods of inclement weather. However, since the Flag Code speaks in terms of 'days when the weather is inclement,' it apparently does not contemplate that on an otherwise fair day, Our Flag should be lowered during brief periods of precipitation occurring that day.

Position and Manner of Display

Our Flag, when carried in a procession with another flag or flags, should be either on the marching right; that is, the Flag's own right, or, if there is a line of other flags, in front of the center of that line.

(a) Our Flag should not be displayed on a float in a parade, except from a staff, or as provided in subsection (i) of this section.

(b) Our Flag should not be draped over the hood, top, sides or back of a vehicle or of a train or a boat. When Our Flag is displayed on an automobile, the staff shall be fixed firmly to the chassis or clamped to the right fender.

(c) No other flag or pennant should be placed above or, if on the same level, to the right of the Flag of the United States of America, except during church services conducted by naval chaplains at sea, when the church pennant may be flown above the Flag during church services for the personnel of the Navy. No person shall display the flag of the United Nations or any other national or international flag equal, above or in a position of superior prominence or honor to or in place of the Flag of the United States, except in the case of the flag of the United Nations, which is flown in a superior position to national flags at the headquarters of the United Nations.

(d) The Flag of the United States of America, when it is displayed with another flag against a wall from crossed staffs, should be in front of the staff of the other flag.

(e) The Flag of the United States of America should be at the center and at the highest point of the group when a number of flags of states or localities or pennants of societies are grouped and displayed from staffs.

(f) When flags of states, cities or localities, or pennants of societies are flown on the same halyard with the Flag of the United States, the latter should always be at the peak. When the flags are flown from adjacent staffs, the Flag of the United States should be hoisted first and lowered last. No such flag or pennant may be placed above the Flag of the United States or to the United States Flag's right.

(g) When flags of two or more nations are displayed, they are to be flown from separate staffs of the same height. The flags should be of approximately equal size. International usage for-

Above: The Vietnam Memorial in Washington, DC with the Lincoln Memorial in the background.

Although there are only eight places (*see text, these pages*) where Our Flag may be flown at night under specific legal authority, it is generally accepted that The Flag may be flown elsewhere if it is properly lighted and displayed in the spirit of the Flag Code.

bids the display of the flag of one nation above that of another nation in time of peace.

(h) When the Flag of the United States is displayed from a staff projecting horizontally or at an angle from the window sill, balcony or front of a building, the union of Our Flag should be placed at the peak of the staff, unless the flag is at half-staff. When Our Flag is suspended over a sidewalk from a rope extending from a house to a pole at the edge of the sidewalk, the Flag should be hoisted out, union first, from the building.

(i) When displayed either horizontally or vertically against a wall, the union should be uppermost and to Our Flag's own right, that is, to the observer's left. When displayed in a window, Our Flag should be displayed in the same way, with the union or blue field to the left of the observer in the street.

(j) When Our Flag is displayed over the middle of the street, it should be suspended vertically with the union to the north in an east and west street or to the east in a north and south street.

(k) When used on a speaker's platform, Our Flag, if displayed flat, should be displayed above and behind the speaker. When displayed from a staff in a church or public auditorium, the Flag of the United States of America should hold the position of superior prominence, in advance of the audience, and in the position of honor at the clergyman's or speaker's right as he faces the audience. Any other flag so displayed should be placed on the left of the clergyman or speaker or to the right of the audience.

(l) Our Flag should form a distinctive feature of the ceremony of unveiling a statue or monument, but it should never be used as the covering for the statue or monument.

Below: When Our Flag is displayed horizontally behind a speaker—such as President Jimmy Carter as seen here—the field of blue, or union, should be uppermost and to the speaker's right.

(m) Our Flag, when flown at half-staff, should be first hoisted to the peak for an instant and then lowered to the half-staff position. The Flag should be again raised to the peak before it is lowered for the day. On Memorial Day, the Flag should be displayed at half-staff until noon only, then raised to the top of the staff. By order of the President, the Flag shall be flown at half-staff upon the death of principal figures of the United States government and the governor of a state, territory or possession, as a mark of respect to their memory. In the event of the death of other officials or foreign dignitaries, the Flag is to be displayed at half-staff according to presidential instructions or orders, or in accordance with recognized customs or practices not inconsistent with law. In the event of the death of a present or former official of the government of any state, territory, or possession of the United States, the governor of that state, territory or possession may proclaim that the National Flag shall be flown at half-staff. The Flag shall be flown at half-staff 30 days from the death of the President or a former President; 10 days from the day of death of the Vice President, the Chief Justice or a retired Chief Justice of the United States or the Speaker of the House of Representatives; from the day of death until interment of an Associate Justice of the Supreme Court, a Secretary of an executive or military department, a former Vice President or governor of a state, territory or possession; and on the day of death and the following day for a member of Congress. The term 'half-staff' means the position of Our Flag when it is one-half the distance between the top and bottom of the staff. The term 'member of Congress' means a sena-

Below: Red, white and blue bunting—as seen in this photograph taken at Mokelumne Hill, California on 4 July 1976—is often used in celebrations of Flag Day, the Fourth of July or, in this case, our nation's bicentennial.

tor, a representative, a delegate or the resident commissioner from Puerto Rico.

(n) When Our Flag is used to cover a casket, it should be so placed that the union is at the head and over the left shoulder. The Flag should not be lowered into the grave or allowed to touch the ground.

(o) When Our Flag is suspended across a corridor or lobby in a building with only one main entrance, it should be suspended vertically, with the union of the Flag to the observer's left upon entering. If the building has more then one main entrance, the flag should be suspended vertically near the center of the corridor or lobby, with the union to the north, when entrances are to the east and west or to the east when entrances are to the north and south. If there are entrances in more than two directions, the union should be to the east.

The amendments made by Public Law 93-344 to Section 3(m) of the Flag Code set out detailed instructions as to the occasions and manner of flying the Flag at half-staff on Memorial Day and as a mark of respect to the memory of certain recently deceased individuals. The new language embodies the substance of Presidential Proclamation 3044 (1 March 1954), entitled 'Display of Flag at Half-Staff Upon Death of Certain Officials and Former Officials.'

Section 3(m) now provides that the President shall order the flag flown at half-staff for stipulated periods 'upon the death of principal figures of the United States government and the governor of a state, territory or possession.' After the death of other officials or foreign dignitaries, the flag may be flown at half-staff according to presidential instructions or in accordance with recognized custom not inconsistent with law. In addition, the Governor of a state, territory or possession may direct that the National Flag be flown at half-staff

Below: These World War I soldiers are about to ship out to overseas posts and this gathering was planned by the women in their community in their honor.

in the event of the death of a present or former official of the respective government.

Presidents have issued orders to fly the flag at half-staff on the death of leading citizens, not covered by law, as a mark of official tribute to their service to the United States. Martin Luther King, Jr is among those who have been so honored.

It should be noted that although Section 3(m) may serve as a guide, this section does not apply, as a matter of law, to the display of the Flag at half-staff by private individuals and organizations. No federal restrictions or court decisions are known that limit such an individual's lowering his own flag or that make such display alone a form of desecration.

Respect for our Flag

(a) No disrespect should be shown to the Flag of the United States of America; the Flag should not be dipped to any person or thing. Regimental colors,

state flags and organization or institutional flags are to be dipped as a mark of honor.

(b) Our Flag should never touch anything beneath it, such as the ground, the floor, water or merchandise.

(c) Our Flag should never be carried flat or horizontally, but always aloft and free.

(d) Our Flag should never be used as wearing apparel, bedding or drapery. It should never be festooned, drawn back, nor up, in folds, but always allowed to fall free. Bunting of blue, white and red, always arranged with the blue above, the white in the middle and the red below, should be used for covering a speaker's desk, draping the front of the platform and for decoration in general.

(e) Our Flag should never be fastened, displayed, used or stored in such a manner as to permit it to be easily torn, soiled or damaged in any way.

(f) Our Flag should never be used as a covering for a ceiling.

(g) Our Flag should never have placed upon it, nor on any part of it, nor attached to it any mark, insignia, letter, word, figure, design, picture or drawing of any nature.

(h) Our Flag should never be used as a receptacle for receiving, holding, carrying or delivering anything.

(i) Our Flag should never be used for advertising purposes in any manner whatsoever. It should not be embroidered on such articles as cushions or handkerchiefs and the like, printed or otherwise impressed on paper napkins or boxes or anything that is designed for temporary use and discard. Advertising signs should not be fastened to a staff or halyard from which the Flag is flown.

(j) No part of Our Flag should ever be used as a costume or athletic uniform. However, a flag patch is often affixed to the uniforms of professional sports teams and frequently to the uniforms of military personnel, firemen, policemen and members of patriotic organizations.

Our Flag represents a living country and is itself considered a living thing. Therefore, the lapel flag pin being a replica, should be worn on the left lapel near the heart.

(k) Our Flag, when it is in such condition that it is no longer a fitting emblem for display, should be destroyed in a dignified way, preferably by burning.

Above: Wrong! Although their hearts are in the right place, these people are in violation of the Flag Code. Our Flag should never be used as wearing apparel, nor have any other images superimposed over it.

Below: This colorful assemblage of 50-star American Flags was displayed by the National Hotel in San Andreas, California in celebration of our nation's bicentennial in 1976.

Opposite page: The display of patriotism during our bicentennial in 1976 was superseded by that which occurred when the nation went to war in 1991. Flags sprouted on every street in the land, and Alvarado Street in San Francisco was no exception.

The Flag Code is silent as to ornaments (finials) for flagstaffs. There appears to be no law or regulation which restricts the use of a finial on the staff. The eagle finial is used not only by the President, the Vice President and many other federal agencies, but also by many civilian organizations and private citizens. The selection of the type finial used is a matter of preference of the individual or organization.

The placing of a fringe on Our Flag is optional with the person or organization, and no Act of Congress or Executive Order either requires or prohibits the practice, according to the Institute of Heraldry.

Fringe is used on indoor flags only, as fringe on flags used outdoors would deteriorate rapidly. The fringe on a Flag is considered an 'honorable enrichment only,' and its official use by the US Army dates from 1895. A 1925 Attorney General's Opinion states: 'The fringe does not appear to be regarded as an integral part of the Flag, and its presence cannot be said to constitute an unauthorized addition to the design prescribed by statute. An external fringe is to be distinguished from letters, words or emblematic designs printed or superimposed upon the body of the flag itself. Under the law, such additions might be open to objection as unauthorized; but the same is not necessarily true of the fringe.'

The Flag Act is silent as to any prescribed act or procedure to be followed in, or in connection with, the burning of a flag. it would seem that any procedure which is in good taste and shows no disrespect to Our Flag would be appropriate. The Flag Protection Act of 1989, struck down albeit on grounds unrelated to this specific point, prohibited *inter alia* 'knowingly' burning a Flag of the United States, but excepted from prohibition 'any conduct consisting of disposal of a flag when it has become worn or soiled.'

Sections 3(c) and 3(g) of the Flag Code provide the rules relating to the position that the National Flag should occupy when displayed with other flags. The meaning of Section 3 can be summarized in one sentence: The Flag of the United States should always be displayed with utmost dignity and respect, and in the position of highest honor. For this purpose, the Flag Code lists several alternate ways in which the flag may be displayed with other flags which will preserve the honor to be accorded it.

Section 3(c) indicates that no flag, other than a church flag during services at sea, should be displayed above the United States Flag. If all the flags are displayed at the same height, the United States Flag is to be given a place of superior prominence, to the right of other flags. This section does not require the federal Flag to be flown higher than any other flag, so long as no flag is above it, but does require it to be flown to the right of all other flags if it is not above them. By international custom, flags of all nations are to be flown at the same height when displayed together; therefore, the part of Section 3(c) dealing with the display of flags at the same height is designed to comply with the respect to be accorded all nations when the United States Flag is displayed with the flags of

Above: Family members have said their good-byes and watch as soldiers of the 24th Infantry Division depart to Saudi Arabia for Operation *Desert Shield* in 1990.

Below: Celebrating the history of the United States, both the Stars and Stripes and the Stars and Bars are proudly displayed at the Silver Spurs Rodeo in Kissimmee, Florida. The Stars and Stripes is, of course, positioned to the right of Miss Silver Spurs and her colleagues.

Facing page: When the American Flag is flown *between* two other flags it should always be on a taller pole. The flag in the foreground is the state flag of Tennessee.

other nations. An exception is made for display of the United States Flag at the United Nations Headquarters in New York. At that site, the United Nations flag may be displayed at a position of superior prominence.

Section 3(e) deals with the situation when the United States Flag is displayed with the flags of states of the Union or municipalities and not with the flags of other nations. In this case, the federal Flag, which represents all states, should be flown above and at the center of the other flags.

Section 3(f) is in accord with Section 3(e), but deals with the special situation when there is only one flagpole, but other state or municipal flags are to be displayed with the federal Flag. In this case, the federal Flag should be displayed above the other flags.

Section 3(g) reiterates the provision of Section 3(c) respecting the position of the United States Flag in relation to flags of other nations. This subsection further elaborates the proper manner of display in such a situation: flags of different nations should be of approximately equal size and flown from the same height.

Section 4(i) and 4(j) address the impropriety of using Our Flag as an article of personal adornment, a design on items of

temporary use, an item of clothing and a means of advertising. The evident purpose of these suggested restraints is to limit the commercial or common usage of Our Flag, and thus maintain its dignity. Section 1(16) of Public Letter 94-344 added language recognizing the wearing of a Flag patch or pin on the left side (near the heart) of uniforms of military personnel, firemen, policemen and members of patriotic organizations.

While the wearing of the colors may be in poor taste and offensive to many, this act alone would not necessarily violate the law. It is questionable whether the wearing of clothing bearing or resembling a Flag, unaccompanied by any other act showing that such use is meant to cast contempt on Our Flag, would be a violation of any flag desecration laws.

Section 4(i) states in part that 'The Flag should never be used for advertising purposes in any manner whatsoever.' As with the rest of the Flag Code, this statement is intended as a guide to be followed on a purely voluntary basis to insure proper respect for Our Flag.

Prohibitions on the use of Our Flag for advertising purposes in the District of Columbia are found in 4 US Code Section 3. States also may restrict use of pictures of the Flag on commercial products.

Conduct During Hoisting, Lowering or Passing of the Flag

During the ceremony of hoisting or lowering Our Flag or when Our Flag is passing in a parade or in review, all persons present, except those in uniform, should face the Flag and stand at attention with the right hand over the heart. Those present in uniform should render the military salute. When not in uniform, men should remove their hats with their right hand and hold them at the left shoulder, the hand being over the heart. Aliens should stand at attention. The salute to Our Flag in a moving column should be rendered at the moment Our Flag passes.

Modification of Rules and Customs by the President

Any rule or custom pertaining to the display of Our Flag of the United States of America, set forth herein, may be altered, modified or repealed, or additional rules with respect thereto may be prescribed by the Commander-in-Chief of the Armed Forces of the United States, whenever he deems it to be appropriate or desirable; and any such alteration or additional rule shall be set forth in a proclamation.

THE LITERATURE OF OUR FLAG

Below: During Operation *Desert Storm* in 1991, this Tillamook, Oregon shop posted small flags for each of the local men and women who had gone overseas.

Facing page: Private TP Loughlin of the 69th Regiment of the New York National Guard (165th Infantry) bidding his family an emotional farewell before he leaves for war in 1917.

A s the symbol of a nation, a flag is as much a thing of the spirit as it is a thing of cloth. Through the years, Our Flag has been the object of numerous tributes in both prose and poetry.

In *The Literature of Our Flag*, we have endeavored to bring together some notable examples of that literature, some well known—indeed immortal, such as *The Star-Spangled Banner*—and others which are more obscure. All, however, are alike in their singular purpose: to honor Our Flag.

THE AMERICAN FLAG

Joseph Rodman Drake

When freedom, from her mountain
    height,
Unfurled her standard to the air,
She tore the azure robe of night,
And set the stars of glory there.
She mingled with its gorgeous dyes
The milky baldric of the skies,
Then from his mansion in the sun
She called her eagle-bearer down
And gave into his mighty hand
The symbol of her chosen land.

THE FLAG GOES BY

Henry Holcomb Bennett

Hats off!
Along the street there comes
A blare of bugles, a ruffle of drums,
A flash of color beneath the sky:
    Hats off!
The flag is passing by!
Blue and crimson and white it shines,
Over the steel-tipped, ordered lines.
    Hats off!
The colors before us fly;
But more than the flag is passing by.

Sea-fights and land-fights, grim and
    great,
Fought to make and to save the State:
Weary marches and sinking ships;
Cheers of victory on dying lips;

Days of plenty and years of peace;
March of a strong land's swift increase;
Equal justice, right, and law,
Stately honor and reverent awe;

Sign of a nation, great and strong
To ward her people from foreign
    wrong:
Pride and glory and honor—all
Live in the colors to stand or fall.

    Hats off!
Along the street there comes
A blare of bugles, a ruffle of drums,
And loyal hearts are beating high:
    Hats off!
The flag is passing by!

Right: The Independence Day Parade in Moscow, Vermont as photographed by Michael Clark in 1989.

MAKERS OF THE FLAG

Franklin K Lane

(From an address delivered by Franklin K Lane, Secretary of the Interior, before more than 1000 employees of the Department of the Interior on Flag Day, 14 June 1914).

This morning, as I passed into the Land Office, the Flag dropped me a most cordial salutation, and from its rippling folds I heard it say: 'Good morning, Mr Flag Maker.'

'I beg your pardon, Old Glory,' I said. 'Aren't you mistaken? I am not the President of the United States, nor a member of Congress, nor even a general in the Army. I am only a government clerk.'

'I greet you again, Mr Flag Maker,' replied the cheerful voice. 'I know you well. You are the man who worked in the swelter of yesterday, straightening out the tangle of that farmer's homestead in Idaho, or perhaps you found the mistake in that Indian contract in Oklahoma, or helped to clear that patent for a hopeful inventor in New York, or pushed the opening of that new ditch in Colorado, or made that mine in Illinois more safe, or brought relief to the old soldier in Wyoming. No matter: whatever one of these beneficent individuals you happen to be, I give you greeting, Mr Flag Maker.'

I was about to pass on, when the Flag stopped me with these words:

'Yesterday the President spoke a word that made happier the future of ten million peons in Mexico; but that act looms no larger on the Flag than the struggle which the boy in Georgia is making to win the Corn Club prize this summer.

'Yesterday the Congress spoke a word which will open the door of Alaska; but a mother in Michigan worked from sunrise until far into the night, to give her boy an

Below: In 1918, these elderly immigrant women did their part for the United States during wartime by sewing Flags. Their Flag-making instructor, Rose Radin, is standing.

education. She, too, is making the Flag.

'Yesterday we made a new law to prevent financial panics, and yesterday, maybe a schoolteacher in Ohio taught his first letters to a boy who will one day write a song that will give cheer to the millions of our race. We are all making the Flag.'

'But,' I said impatiently, 'these people were only working!'

Then came a great shout from the Flag:

'The work that we do is the making of the Flag.

'I am not the Flag; not at all. I am but its shadow.

'I am whatever you make me, nothing more.

'I am your belief in yourself, your dream of what a people may become.

'I live a changing life, a life of moods and passions, of heartbreaks and tired muscles.

'Sometimes I am strong with pride, when men do an honest work, fitting the rails together truly.

'Sometimes I droop, for then purpose has gone from me, and cynically I play the coward.

'Sometimes I am loud, garish and full of ego that blasts judgment.

'But always, I am all that you hope to be, and have the courage to try for.

'I am song and fear, struggle and panic, and ennobling hope.

'I am the day's work of the weakest man and the largest dream of the most daring.

'I am the Constitution and the courts, statutes and state-maker, soldier and dreadnaught, drayman and sweep, cook, counselor and clerk.

'I am the battle of yesterday and the mistake of tomorrow.

'I am the mystery of the men who do without knowing why.

'I am the clutch of an idea and the reasoned purpose of resolution.

'I am no more than what you believe me to be and I am all that you believe I can be.

'I am what you make me; nothing more.

'I swing before your eyes as a bright gleam of color, a symbol of yourself, the pictured suggestion of that big thing which makes this nation. My stars and my stripes are your dreams and your labors. They are bright with cheer, brilliant with courage, firm with faith, because you have made them so out of your hearts; for you are the makers of the Flag, and it is well that you glory in the making.'

Below: Our Flag—a symbol of the beliefs, dreams and labors of the American people.

THE MEANING OF OUR FLAG

Henry Ward Beecher

If one asks me the meaning of our flag, I say to him: It means just what Concord and Lexington meant, what Bunker Hill meant. It means the whole glorious Revolutionary War. It means all that the Declaration of Independence meant. It means all that the Constitution of our people, organizing for justice, for liberty and for happiness, meant.

Under this banner rode Washington and his armies. Before it Burgoyne laid down his arms. It waved on the highlands at West Point. When Arnold would have surrendered these valuable fortresses and precious legacies, his night was turned into day and his treachery was driven away by beams of light from this starry banner.

It cheered our Army, driven out from around New York, and in their painful pilgrimages through New Jersey. This banner streamed in light over the soldiers' heads at Valley Forge and at Morristown. It crossed the waters rolling with ice at Trenton, and when its stars gleamed in the cold morning with a victory, a new day of hope dawned on the despondency of this nation.

Our Flag carries American ideas, American history and American feelings. Beginning with the Colonies, and coming down to our time, in its sacred heraldry, in its glorious insignia, it has gathered and stored chiefly this supreme idea: *divine right of liberty in man*. Every color means liberty; every thread means liberty; every form of star and beam or stripe of light means liberty—not lawlessness, not license, but organized, institutional liberty—liberty through law, and laws for liberty!

This American Flag was the safeguard of liberty. Not an atom of crown was allowed to go into its insignia. Not a symbol of authority in the ruler was permitted to go into it. It was an ordinance of liberty by the people, for the people. That it meant, that it means, and, by the blessing of God, that it shall mean to the end of time!

Right: A flurry of Flags and patriotism at the annual Orange Bowl Parade in Florida.
Page 64: This 34-star Flag is being used in a recreation of a Civil War battle.
Page 65: Nothing but Flags: The arc of Old Glories that surround the Washington Monument in Washington, DC.

THE NAME OF OLD GLORY

James Whitcomb Riley

Old Glory! say, who—
By the ship and the crew,
And the long blended ranks of the gray
   and the blue—

Who gave you, Old Glory, the name
   that you bear
With such pride everywhere
As you cast yourself free to the
   rapturous air
And leap out full-length, as we're
   wanting you to?
Who gave you that name with the ring
   of the same
And the honor and fame so becoming
   to you?
Your stripes stroked in ripples of white
   and of red,
With your stars at their glittering best
   overhead—
     By day or by night
     Their delightful light

Laughing down from their square of
   heaven of blue!
Who gave you the name of Old
   Glory?—say, who—
Who gave you the name of Old Glory?

The old banner lifted, and faltering
   then,
In vague lisps and whispers fell
   silent again.

Old Glory—speak out! We are asking
   about
How you happened to 'favor' a name,
   so to say,
That's so familiar and careless and gay
As we cheer it and shout in our wild,
   breezy way—
We—the crowd, every man of us
   calling you that—
We—Tom, Dick and Harry—each
   swinging his hat
And hurrahing 'Old Glory!' like you
   were our kin,
When—Lord!—we all know we're as
   common as sin!
And waft us your thanks, as we hail
   you and fall
Into line, with you over us, waving us
   on
Where our glorified, sanctified betters
   have gone.
And this is the reason we're wanting to
   know—

(And we're wanting it *so*!—
Where our fathers went we are willing
   to go.)
Who gave you the name of Old Glory—
   Oho!—
Who gave you the name of Old Glory?
     The old flag unfurled with a
      billowy thrill
     For an instant, then wistfully
      sighed and was still.

Old Glory, the story we're wanting to
   hear
Is what the plain facts of your
   christening were—
For your name—just to hear it,
Repeat it and cheer it, 'tis a tang to the
   spirit
As salt as a tear—
And seeing you fly, and the boys
   passing by,
There's a shout in the throat and a blur
   in the eye,
And an aching to live for you always—
   or die,
If, dying, we still keep you waving on
   high.
     And so, by our love
     For you, floating above,

And the scars of all wars and the
   sorrows thereof,
Who gave you the name of Old Glory,
   and why
Are we thrilled at the name of Old
   Glory?
     Then the old banner leaped like a
      sail in the blast,
     And fluttered an audible answer at
      last.

And it spake with a shake of the voice,
   and it said:
By the driven snow-white and the
   living blood-red
Of my bars, and their heaven of stars
   overhead—
By the symbol conjoin of them,
   skyward cast,
As I float from the steeple or flap at the
   mast,
Or droop o'er the sod where long
   grasses nod—
My name is as old as the Glory of God.
So I came by the name of Old Glory.

NOTHING BUT FLAGS

Moses A Owen

Nothing but flags—but simple flags,
Tattered and torn and hanging in rags;
And we walk beneath them with
   careless tread,
Nor think of the host of the mighty
   dead,
That have marched beneath them in
   days gone by,
With a burning cheek and a kindling
   eye,
And have bathed their folds with their
   young life's tide,
And, dying, blessed them, and blessing,
   died.

Nothing but flags—yet methinks at
   night
They tell each other their tales of
   fright;

And dim specters come and their thin
   arms twine
'Round each standard torn, as they
   stand in line!
As the word is given—they charge!
   they form!
And the dim hall rings with the battle's
   storm!
And once again through the smoke and
   strife
Those colors lead to a nation's life.

Nothing but flags—yet, bathed with
   tears,
They tell of triumphs, of hopes of fears;
Of earnest prayers for the absent men,
Of the battlefield and the prison pen;
Silent, they speak; and the tear will
   start

As we stand before them with
   throbbing heart,
And think of those who are not forgot;
Their flags came hither—but they
   came not.

Nothing but flags—yet we hold our
   breath
And gaze with awe at these types of
   death;
Nothing but flags—yet the thought will
   come,
The heart must pray though the lips
   are dumb.
They are sacred, pure, and we see no
   stain
Of those loved flags, which came home
   again;
Baptized in blood of our purest, best,
Tattered and torn, they are now at rest.

OLD GLORY

Maximilian Beyer

My Flag! Immortal emblem of our
  faith,
Born in the travail of creating time,
Your beacon stars, majestic and
  sublime,
Blaze through the ages freedom's
  glorious path.
We bow in reverence to your field of
  red,
Cleft by the gleaming white of liberty,
Our equal crown, wrought by eternity
To that great host of our heroic dead.
Enthroned in your starlit azure blue,
Summons our Union's lofty destiny.
Your sons and daughters—O
  Democracy!
To guard their trust and to your faith
  be true:
The Faith wrought right, caught from
  heaven's starry plain,
That wreathes in glory your
  triumphant reign.

OLD GLORY

Alonzo Newton Benn

I love each shining star because
  It tells a wondrous story;
I love each stripe no whit the less
  And shall as I grow hoary!

I love its field of azure blue
  Wherein each star does twinkle;
I love its red and snowy white
  And every fold and wrinkle!

I love to see it float on high
  Above each tower and steeple;
I love to doff my hat to it;
  The Flag of a free people!

I love Old Glory more each day,
  The banner of our nation;
The grandest country in the world,
  The best of God's creation!

Right: A Memorial Day tribute at an American cemetery.

OUR COUNTRY'S FLAG

William Dawson

Flag of an empire vast and free,
    Flag of a people's liberty:
Flag of our hopes, flag ever true,
    Flag of our hearts, red, white and
        blue.
Flag of the brave, the hero's pride,
    Flag forever to be our guide:
Flag of the stars, flag of the dawn—
    Flag of a hemisphere's new morn.

Flag of the rich, flag of the poor,
    Flag of us all from shore to shore:
Flag of democracy's decree—
    Flag of our nation's entity.

Flag made sacred by sacrifice,
    Flag that has known no
        compromise:
Flag of the truth, we see in thee—
    Flag of eternal victory.

Flag of our country, winsome, fair,
    Flag of free men everywhere:
Flag superb and the flag supreme—
    Flag of the whole world's noblest
        dream.
Flag we salute, the flag we love,
    Flag given to us by God above:
Flag of the East, Flag of the West—
    Flag of all flags, thou are the best!

Above: These US Army personnel pose for a photo in Saudi Arabia during Operation *Desert Shield* in 1991.

Right: Two enlisted men of the ill-fated US Navy aircraft carrier *Liscome Bay* are buried at sea from the deck of a Coast Guard-manned assault transport. The *Liscome Bay* was sunk in November 1943 during World War II.

OUR FLAG

Lydia Avery Coonley Ward

There are many flags in many lands,
　　There are flags of every hue,
But there is no flag, however grand,
　　Like our own 'Red, White and Blue.'
I know where the prettiest colors are;
　　And I'm sure if I only knew
How to get them here, I could make a
　　flag
　　Of glorious 'Red, White and Blue.'

I would cut a piece from an evening
　　sky,
　　Where the stars are shining
　　　through,
And use it just as it was on high,
　　For my stars and field of blue.

Then I'd want a part of a fleecy cloud,
　　And some red from a rainbow
　　　bright;
And put them together side by side,
　　For my stripes of red and white.

We shall always love the 'Stars and
　　Stripes,'
　　And we mean to be ever true
To this land of ours and the dear old
　　flag,
　　The Red, the White and the Blue.

Then hurrah for the flag! our country's
　　flag;
　　Its stripes and white stars too.
There is no flag in any land
　　Like our own 'Red, White and Blue.'

Above: Our Flag flies in victory in the 1984 Olympic basketball finals.

Facing page: Our Flag waves proudly above schools and civic buildings in every city, town and village across the United States.

THE SCHOOLHOUSE STANDS BY THE FLAG

Hezekiah Butterworth

Ye who love the Republic, remember the claim
Ye owe to her fortunes, ye owe to her name.
To her years of prosperity past and in store,
A hundred behind you, a thousand before.

The blue arch above us in liberty's dome,
The green fields beneath us equality's home,
But the schoolroom today is humanity's friend—
Let the people, the flag and the schoolhouse defend.

'Tis the schoolhouse that stands by the flag,
    Let the nation stand by the school;
'Tis the school bell that rings for our liberty old,
    'Tis the schoolboy whose ballot shall rule.

THE STAR-SPANGLED BANNER

Francis Scott Key

O say can you see by the dawn's early
light,
What so proudly we hail'd at the
twilight's last gleaming,
Whose broad stripes and bright stars,
through the perilous fight,
O'er the ramparts we watch'd were so
gallantly streaming?
And the rocket's red glare, the bomb
bursting in air,
Gave proof through the night that our
flag was still there.
Oh, say, does that star-spangled
banner yet wave
O'er the land of the free and the home
of the brave?

On the shore, dimly seen through the
mists of the deep,
Where the foe's haughty host in dread
silence reposes,
What is that which the breeze, o'er the
towering steep,
As it fitfully blows, half conceals, half
discloses?
Now it catches the gleam of the
morning's first beam,
In full glory reflected now shines on
the stream.
'Tis the star-spangled banner—o long
may it wave
O'er the land of the free and the home
of the brave!

Oh, thus be it ever when freemen shall
stand
Between their lov'd homes and the
war's desolation!
Blest with vict'ry and peace, may the
heav'n rescued land
Praise the pow'r that hath made and
preserved us a nation!
Then conquer we must, when our
cause it is just,
And this be our motto: 'In God is our
Trust.'
And the star-spangled banner in
triumph shall wave
O'er the land of the free and the home
of the brave.

FLAGS OF

Alabama

Alaska

Arizona

Arkansas

California

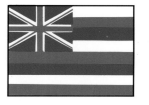

Hawaii

Idaho

Illinois

Indiana

Iowa

Massachusetts

Michigan

Minnesota

Mississippi

Missouri

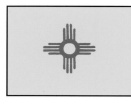

New Mexico

New York

North Carolina

North Dakota

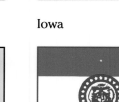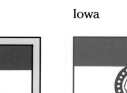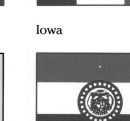

Ohio

South Dakota

Tennessee

Texas

Utah

Vermont

District of Columbia

Guam

Puerto Rico

OUR STATES

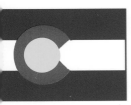

Colorado

Connecticut

Delaware

Florida

Georgia

Kansas

Kentucky

Louisiana

Maine

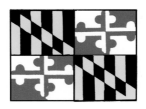

Maryland

Montana

Nebraska

Nevada

New Hampshire

New Jersey

Oklahoma

Oregon

Pennsylvania

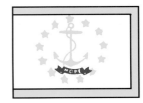

Rhode Island

South Carolina

Virginia

Washington

West Virginia

Wisconsin

Wyoming

Pacific Islands

Virgin Islands

American Samoa

GLOSSARY

Band: A narrow strip of canvas along the edge of the flag that goes next to the staff. Sometimes called 'heading.'

Canton: The rectangular space occupied in the American Flag by the blue field. In day-to-day use, in referring to the American Flag the words 'union' and 'canton' are used interchangeably.

Color: In the military service, a national flag carried by unmounted units is called a color. The expression 'the colors' is used quite generally in referring to a flag.

Dip: To dip a flag is to lower it in salute.

Ensign: In its navy, a national flag is usually called an ensign. Often naval ensigns are variations on a national flag.

Fringe: A yellow border around the flag.

Fly: The side of a flag extending from the staff to the flying end—that is, the long side.

Grommet: The eyelet through which the halyard is fastened to a flag.

Half-Mast/ Half-Staff: To half-mast or half-staff a flag is to lower it some distance (though not necessarily halfway down) from the top of the flagpole, as a token of mourning. The terms half-mast and half-staff are used interchangeably, although 'half-mast' is used almost exclusively in the US Navy.

Halyard: A rope or cord with which a flag is drawn to the top of its staff, and with which it is lowered.

Heading: See 'band.'

Hoist: The hoist of a flag is the side extending along the staff—that is, the short side. To hoist a flag is to raise it to the top of the staff.

Peak: The highest point to which a flag can be raised. The top of a ball, or end of a spike topping a flagstaff is, therefore, not the peak of the staff.

Standard: A national flag when carried in military service by mounted or motorized units.

Strike: To strike a flag is to haul it down in token of surrender.

Union: The union of the Flag of the United States is the cluster of 50 stars, on the field of blue, symbolizing the union of the states.

INDEX

Facing page: An enormous Flag forms the centerpiece of a parade in Illinois.

Page 79: A Marine honor guard strikes the colors aboard the USS *New Jersey*.

Page 80: Our Flag flies over the Presidio National Cemetery in San Francisco.

Flag Anniversaries

1 January: The Grand Union Flag, the first flag of the United Colonies, was hoisted for the first time at Prospect Hill, near Washington's headquarters at Cambridge, Massachusetts in 1776.

13 January: By an Act of Congress in 1794, two stars and two stripes, representing Vermont and Kentucky, were added to Our Flag, producing a flag of 15 stars and 15 stripes. Under this flag, the United States fought three wars: the Naval War with France in 1798, the war with Tripoli in 1801-5 and the War of 1812 with England.

26 January: In 1813, the frigate USS *Essex*, after rounding Cape Horn, was the first warship to fly the American Flag in the Pacific.

28 January: The first display of the American Flag in an attack against a foreign stronghold was at Nassau in the Bahamas, when the Americans captured Fort Nassau from the British and raised The Stars and Stripes in 1783.

3 February: The first appearance of the American Flag in an English port was when the ship *Bedford* of Massachusetts arrived in England in 1783.

14 February: The first foreign salute to The Stars and Stripes, the new American Flag, was rendered when John Paul Jones, in command of the USS *Ranger*, entered Quiberon Bay, near Brest, France, and received a salute from the French fleet, under Admiral LaMotte Piquet in 1778.

23 February In 1945, during World War II, Associated Press photographer Joe Rosenthal took the most famous photograph of an American Flag raising ever, as Marines hoisted The Stars and Stripes atop Mount Suribachi on Iwo Jima.

6 April: In 1909, Admiral Robert E Peary first planted an American Flag at the North Pole.

24 April: In 1778, John Paul Jones, in command of the USS *Ranger*, achieved the honor of being the first officer of the American Navy to compel a British man-of-war, the HMS *Drake*, to strike her colors to the new American Flag.

27 April: In 1804, the American Flag was raised for the first time over an enemy installation in the Eastern Hemisphere at Derna, Tripoli, during the war between the United States and Tripoli.

14 June: The first Flag of the United States was adopted by Congress in 1777. This date was formally proclaimed as 'Flag Day' in 1916.

2 July: In 1777, The Stars and Stripes was displayed for the first time in the Navy by Captain John Paul Jones, in command of the USS *Ranger*.

4 July: All new stars, since the 16th one in 1818, have been officially added to Our Flag on 4 July. The most recent one to be added was the 50th (Hawaii) in 1960.

20 July: The American Flag was raised for the first time on another body in the Solar System when Neil Armstrong and Edwin Aldrin planted Old Glory in the Sea of Tranquillity on the Moon in 1969.

3 August: The first display of The Stars and Stripes by the Continental Army occurred when the flag was hoisted over Fort Stanwix, New York (the present site of Rome) during an attack by the British in 1777. This flag, according to legend, was an improvised affair made of a soldier's white shirt, a woman's red petticoat and a piece of blue cloth from an officer's cloak.

10 August: The American Flag made its first trip around the world, flying from the ship *Columbia*, which sailed from Boston on 30 September 1787 and returned on this date in 1790.

21 August: In 1960, the 50-star American Flag was officially unfurled for the first time (but not actually raised) by President Dwight Eisenhower in Washington, DC.

11 September: The Stars and Stripes was first carried by troops in battle at Brandywine, Pennsylvania in 1777. It was the first big battle after the adoption of Our Flag by the Continental Congress. The Americans were, sadly, defeated.

14 September: 'By the dawn's early light' on this date in 1814, Francis Scott Key completed *The Star-Spangled Banner*, the song that would become the National Anthem.

17 October: The American Flag was first saluted by the British at the surrender of Burgoyne's Army in 1777.

18 October: In 1876, the American Flag was first officially displayed over Alaska at the capitaol of Sitka when, in the presence of Russian and American troops, the Russian Flag was lowered and the American Flag hoisted.

16 November: The first foreign salute to an American Flag was the salute which was rendered to the Grand Union Flag by the Dutch governor, De Graaff, on the island of St Eustatius, when the brig *Andrea Doria*, commanded by Captain Robinson, was saluted in 1776.

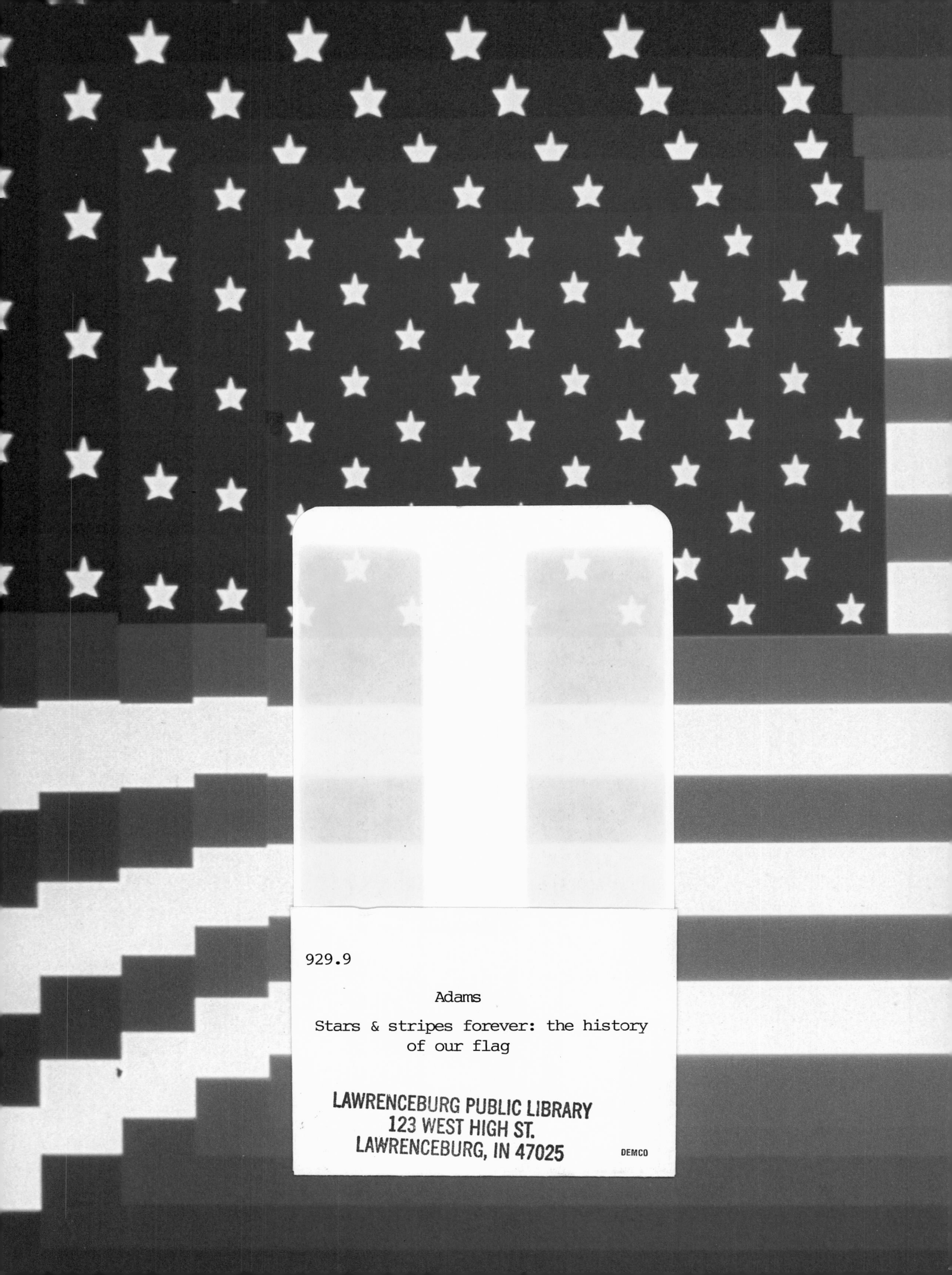